# LORD JIM

# Notes on English Literature

Chief Adviser: JOHN D. JUMP
*Professor of English Literature in the University of Manchester*

General Editor: W. H. MASON
*Lately Senior English Master, Manchester Grammar School*

# LORD JIM
## (CONRAD)

# DOUGLAS L. MENSFORTH

*Research Student of Linacre College, Oxford*

BASIL BLACKWELL
OXFORD

0 631 97990 5

PRINTED IN GREAT BRITAIN BY
WESTERN PRINTING SERVICES LTD, BRISTOL
AND BOUND BY
KEMP HALL BINDERY, OXFORD

# CONTENTS

# GENERAL NOTE

This series of introductions to the great classics of English literature is designed primarily for the school, college, and university student, although it is hoped that they will be found helpful by a much larger audience. Three aims have been kept in mind:

(A) To give the reader the relevant information necessary for his fuller understanding of the work.

(B) To indicate the main areas of critical interest, to suggest suitable critical approaches, and to point out possible critical difficulties.

(C) To do this in as simple and lucid a manner as possible, avoiding technical jargon and giving a full explanation of any critical terms employed.

Each introduction contains questions on the text and suggestions for further reading. It should be emphasized that in no sense is any introduction to be considered as a substitute for the reader's own study, understanding, and appreciation of the work.

# I. SOURCES

*Lord Jim* is a composite work. It is important to recognize from the first the duality of the main sources, in order to understand not only how Conrad has managed to weld them into a coherent and unified whole, but also why he did so, what he was attempting to shew thereby. The figure of Jim is in the original composed of two men, one condemned by a Court of Inquiry for 'officious behaviour and unseamanlike conduct' and of whom the co-judge remarked that he 'should not be permitted to go in the ship again'; the other a successful merchant who became identified with the Malays of his place, Berau, and was indeed known as 'Tuan Jim Lingard'.

On the 20th July, 1880, a vessel called the *Jeddah* left the port of Penang in Malaya (the Straits Settlements) with a complement of a crew of fifty and 992 passengers, bound for the Arabian port of Jedda whence the passengers, Mussulman pilgrims, would proceed over the desert to Mecca. The ship was to await their return to the port and bring them back to the East.

The *Jeddah* was by no means 'as old as the hills, lean like a greyhound, and eaten up with rust worse than a condemned water-tank' as Conrad describes the *Patna* (Chapter II). She was eight years old, and despite having been scuttled off Australia in order to put out a fire six years earlier, had been found *100 A 1* by the Lloyd's surveyor prior to her sailing from Singapore to Penang: this is the highest rating at Lloyd's. In common with almost all steamers of the time, she had provision for sail-power.

Her complement contained seven Europeans: the captain, Joseph Lucas Clark, who was the co-owner of the vessel, and had been master of it on the same pilgrim run for five years; his wife; the first mate, Augustine Podmore Williams, the original of the Lord Jim of the *Patna*; the second mate; and the chief, second and third engineers. The vessel was, as indeed was not uncommon at that time, grossly overloaded; the Court of Inquiry found that it contained 'a greater number than should be allowed by any regulation'. Nevertheless, although it was the monsoon season, she was well-found and seaworthy.

For eighteen days she steamed across the Indian Ocean, attended by the whole range of monsoon weather—as the ship's log shows, five days of hot sun on a calm sea, three days of heavy squalls with rain and wind, five days more of intense sun and heat, and finally five days of gales which eventually broke the ship's mechanism and rendered her derelict.

During the days of the squalls she had sprung various minor leaks, but it was not until the gales struck her, at times with hurricane force, that she began to ship water seriously. On the third of August high seas swept across the decks, and the boilers, two huge masses of metal weighing, full, thirty tons each, broke loose from their mountings and began to slide back and forth by as much as two inches. During the following three days the storms continued, and the movement of the boilers broke the connecting pipes, starting a rapidly increasing leak, putting out the stokehold fires, and rendering the engine-room useless. Captain Clark's report then says:

At 7 a.m. on the same day, the seventh of August, it was still blowing a tremendous gale, and the water in the vessel rose above the fire grates, the boilers started adrift from their seatings, and the stokehole and engine-room plates and bearers dashed about with every roll of the vessel. It now seemed that the vessel had sprung a heavy leak . . .

All hands and passengers turned to the pumps and to baling with buckets; sails were set, which blew away and were replaced. At midnight on the 7th August Captain Clark ordered the boats to be manned which had been swung out since early in the day. But the boats, even if it proved possible to launch them and maintain them afloat in the high seas, could carry but a quarter of the passengers at most, and the pilgrims changed their mood.

At this point, Williams, the Chief Mate, panicked. Believing the vessel to be sinking imminently, he urged upon the captain, a weak and ineffective man, who, in the opinion of the Court, 'shewed a want of judgement and tact to a most serious extent, and . . . caused disorganization and discontent, not to say despair . . .' that they should abandon ship. The argument he used was singular —he represented to the captain that his wife was in imminent danger from the native pilgrims, and that she should be placed for safety in the stern lifeboat. 'The first mate of the *Jeddah*,' said the Court, 'is greatly to blame in doing what he could to demoralize the master.' Williams carried the lady to the lifeboat, and thereafter (again in the words of the Court) 'did thrust the master into the boat'. They were joined by the Chief Engineer, the Third Engineer, and sixteen Malays. Williams remained on the vessel supervising the lowering of the captain's boat, the intention being that he should afterwards take a boat from the port side with the Second Engineer and other

Malay members of the crew. At this juncture, however, the passengers revolted, and, according to Williams's version, threw him over the rails into the sea, where he was picked up by the captain's boat. The question as to whether he had jumped or had been thrown remained dubious at the hearings; one judge said 'Williams found himself in the water', another, 'I believe [the pilgrims] knocked the first mate overboard'; Governor Weld of Singapore, 'Williams says that he was thrown overboard'. Next the pilgrims began to bombard the boat with any convenient missile. Captain Clark later adduced this incident as proof of the contention that the passengers were riotous, but the Court dismissed it as a mere expression of despair. Then the pilgrims turned to the two other lifeboats which were manned; from one, which contained the Second Engineer, they threw the men back into the vessel; the other they cut loose, after the men in it had refused to return, and it sank, drowning all who were in it. The Second Engineer, constrained to remain in the vessel, took charge, but he knew nothing of navigation and the vessel drifted helplessly.

Meanwhile the captain's boat had sailed away; Williams had replied with pistol fire to the bombardment of pots and pans by the pilgrims, and thereafter, although they declared themselves to have remained in the neighbourhood of the ship until dawn, when they said it was not to be seen, the men in the boat took no further interest in the fate of the *Jeddah*. At 10.00 a.m. on the next morning, not seven hours after they had abandoned the vessel, they were sighted and rescued by the Liverpool steamship *Scindia*, which took them to Aden, where Captain Clark, following the agreed story among these survivors, declared his ship to have foundered with the loss of all aboard except themselves. Cables announcing the loss were sent out; such disasters were not uncommon.

The *Jeddah*, however, had not foundered. Moving slowly under sail westward, she was sighted at 4.30 p.m. on the same day by the British steamer *Antenor*, which came to her rescue. In spite of the danger which might be caused to the *Antenor* thereby, it was decided to take the *Jeddah* in tow. (In fact, the engines were overstrained, and the *Antenor* broke down shortly afterwards.) The First Mate of the *Antenor*, Randolph Campbell, was put on board the *Jeddah*, where he remained for sixty-seven hours, seldom leaving the bridge, until they came to Aden. From him Conrad created the figure of the French lieutenant of the *Victorieuse*.

By a curious stroke of irony, the captain of the *Antenor* entered the British Consulate in Aden to report the saving of the *Jeddah* and all aboard at the same moment as Captain Clark was leaving it after having filed his claim for the loss of the vessel. The news of the abandonment and the subsequent rescue aroused enormous public feeling: 'shame', 'disgrace', 'cowardly', 'dastardly' are the leading words used by the newspapers of the period. The Colonial Secretary said, 'The case . . . has affected the whole character of English seamanship throughout the world'.

A Court of Inquiry was convened at Aden. The most remarkable feature of this hearing is the evidence given by Williams, which, far from seeking to exculpate him, served more than anything to incriminate him. He seemed to be determined to seek out suitable punishment.

Williams went out of his way at the hearing in Aden to condemn his own behaviour in the *Jeddah*, but his testimony was unsupported by further evidence, and he was not, in fact, tried, although the findings of the Court administered a severe reprimand which was so worded as to bring about his dismissal. Captain Clark's certificate was not cancelled, but suspended for three years, a sentence whose mildness called forth indignation at the second hearing in Singapore. He held, in fact, one further command, in 1888, but afterwards retired to Australia, where he died in obscurity. Williams, however, took a more extraordinary course.

The case, as we have said, achieved a universal notoriety. It was discussed everywhere, and particularly in the East, where it remained so unforgotten that as late as 1950 the *Straits Times* (Dec. 2nd) could refer to this 'cowardly disregard of the traditions of the sea'. Nevertheless, it was to Singapore, after a year spent drifting about Eastern ports as a water-clerk, that Williams returned, and set himself to live down his reputation. In 1882 he entered the employment of the Singapore firm of ship-chandlers, McAlister and Co., as a water-clerk, in which position he remained for twenty-eight years, afterwards living, at first as a ship-chandler himself, and then, after the failure of this venture, as an employee again. He died in 1916, on the 20th April, having in the thirty-six years of his life in Singapore succeeded in regaining the respect of those who had at the time of the *Jeddah* incident repudiated him, the seamen. Like Jim, he became 'loved, trusted and admired'.

From these materials, then, which were of common knowledge as well in the East as in England, Conrad took his portrait of Jim. The youthful, self-confident, romantically-inclined mate of the *Jeddah*, who had promoted this enormity of the sea, was made into the figure of human weakness and egoism which we see in the former part of *Lord Jim*. Even the details were taken over by Conrad; for Williams's father was indeed a clergyman of the Church of England in possession of the living of Porthleven in Cornwall; and such details as Jim's being owed 'three weeks and five days pay' after leaving the *Patna* were taken from the facts. Conrad met Williams in Singapore, and has included in his portrait of Jim many of the characteristics of the man himself. Nevertheless, important as it is for criticism to know what were the sources from which Conrad took his ideas, of even more importance is it to know what he did with them in transforming them into the finished work of art.

Let us begin by observing one or two minor differences between the novel and the facts of the *Jeddah* case. First, Conrad has made the captain of the *Patna* not an Englishman, as was Clark, but a renegade German, 'very anxious to curse publicly his native country, but who, apparently on the strength of Bismarck's victorious policy, brutalized all those he was not afraid of, and wore a "blood-and-iron" air, combined with a purple nose and a red moustache'. (ii.) Allen suggests that this change was prompted by a desire to avert disgrace from the British Marine on Conrad's part, but this explanation is superficial. Nationality, in the narrow sense, does not matter in the novel: Stein is set as a counterpart to the German captain in order to meet the suggestion which might arise that Conrad is voicing anti-German views. The important thing for Conrad is to stress the wider community, transcending national boundaries, of the sea, and thereby at the same time to show the greater enormity of the crime and to suggest the notion of the wider community, which, as we shall see presently, is eventually made to include all humanity. A similar change is that of Campbell into a French lieutenant. How can this be thought to glorify the British Merchant Service? The explanation is that Conrad is here using the 'Good Samaritan' motif in its original acceptation. Christ told the story of the good Samaritan to confound the Jews; Conrad makes the rescuer French to demonstrate the wider community of human feelings—courage, aid, devotion to duty. This is not to belittle the British—Conrad can be jingoistic enough when he wishes, as in *Heart of Darkness* (q.v.), but here his purpose is other.

What, then, does he make of the figure and the career of Williams? First, the crime is made more definite in the novel. There is no question of the fact of the jumping, except in Jim's own attempts at self-justification and exculpation to Marlow ('I had jumped—it seems'.) The character is naturally more full than it can be in the records, and the interplay of feeling in Jim's mind is of Conrad's creation. But the ending is different. It was not Conrad's intention to make the story of Jim end in his merely working himself back into a position of trust among his former associates, but to present him in another and completely different situation where his characteristics may shew themselves again, whether to the same or to a different end will appear. This is of a piece with his widening conception of the novel. At first he had intended to make nothing more than a yarn of the *Jeddah* story, which would presumably have concluded with the rehabilitation of Jim according to the pattern of Williams; but as the conception of the novel grew in Conrad's mind, he sought another form of expression, for mere rehabilitation was no longer what he wished to present. He therefore took elements from the history of another man altogether, Jim Lingard, an inhabitant of Borneo.

James Lingard was a native of Lancashire, and he was twenty-five, four years younger than Conrad, when the latter met him in Berau in Borneo, which he later made into Patusan. He was a trader who had lived in Borneo for twelve years and had married an Indo-chinese girl by whom he had several children. He was known for his decorous and stately manner, in particular for his rather swaggering walk, 'a dapper person never without his walking stick', as one who knew him said. On account of this he was called 'Gentleman Jim' or 'Lord Jim' by the Europeans who knew him; and this was also his Malay courtesy title, 'Tuan Jim'. Berau was Lingard's home; he spent four-fifths of his life there and came to speak Malay perfectly. There were, however, no startling events in his life there; he was a trader and no more. Nevertheless, Berau was well known, especially to the Dutch authorities, as a trouble-spot, because of the rivalries between the various factions, each with its own rajah, and the Bugis settlers from Celebes. In *Lord Jim* Conrad recalls the regency of Hadji Adji Kuning, when 'Utter insecurity for life and property was the normal condition' and the chaos that prevailed under this ruler, who 'swallowed an opium pill every two hours' made the background for Rajah Allang. Similarly Doramin was a figure founded on one of the leaders of the Bugis merchant settlers. For the Patusan section of the novel, then, the sources are much vaguer; although the characters are based upon Conrad's own knowledge from the days when he was upriver in Borneo, they are much more creations of his own imagination, as is the action. The second part of the novel is of course conceived in regard to the former, and is intended to perform a task much more elaborate than that of a mere yarn, as we shall see when we come to discuss the structure.

## 2. STRUCTURE

The structure of *Lord Jim* has frequently been seen as deficient. It is said that the novel was begun as a simple tale, provoked by the *Jeddah* incident, and that only afterwards did Conrad see its potentialities as a full-length novel; that the Patusan part was subsequently stitched on, from another source, and the whole expanded into an unwieldy and broken-backed composite. The two parts, it is said, are linked tenuously only by the common figure of Jim, and the occasional presence of Marlow—but in reality the two parts are two totally different stories which it is indecorous thus to yoke together. Indeed, one has the feeling that, were this an anonymous mediaeval work, some industrious German would have succeeded by now in proving that the novel was the work of what Tolkien calls 'that well-known committee, A, B, and An Interpolator'. Now this is nothing to the purpose. We are not interested at this stage in the history of the composition of the book. We are to consider it as the whole, in the state in which Conrad left it, and in the state in which he evidently intended it to be read. He seems to have regarded it as complete, and a unity as it now stands. We shall, in fact, find that there is a very carefully constructed and symmetrical structure in *Lord Jim*, where the formal structure points the meaning of the work in a very exact correspondence. Conrad may, perhaps, have begun with the history of the *Jeddah* which he saw would make a good tale, a good short story, and then seen wider applications, but this is not to say that his structure is merely that of two tales tacked together. We shall see certain ways in which explicit parallels are drawn in structure and in language between the two parts of the book: and I think that we should regard the Patusan section as placing Jim in a wider, though related, context than that of the *Patna* or of his sea-training. If Patusan be a chance given to Jim to rehabilitate himself (or not, as the case may be) the change of circumstances indicates a certain change of the terms of the test.

The basic plan of the book is obvious: there is one main part up to Marlow's visit to Stein; and this part is confused in the relation and not perspicuous as to chronology. This technique we shall discuss presently. Thereafter, there is another movement begun, which comprises the Patusan section; and here the narration becomes steadily less confused and more inevitable in its movement towards the end. There are thus two main parts which call for comparison, two principal experiences of Jim which are set against each other. This is the structure at its simplest. Beyond that, of course, the subsidiary incidents fit into this broad scheme by way of leading up to or explaining the principal incidents. All this is done in very symmetrical fashion.

One of the guidelines, one of the leading motifs in the structure of the novel, is the contrast between illusion and reality. This may be seen stylistically, for example, in the descriptions of the illusory calm of the Eastern seas, which conceal at the same time danger and corruption. Similarly, on a larger scale, the first part of the book deals with the revelation of Jim's self-delusion. There are four main crises in the action: the incident in the training-ship, where Jim has for the first time the experience of being overwhelmed by the illusory forces of nature, and subsequently justifying his own inaction to himself and, indeed,

B

drawing fresh self-confidence from it. He regards the incident as a piece of evil luck; indeed, he sees the elements as malevolent in their desire to prevent his gaining the glory which he regards as rightfully his. This is to become one of his principal failings, in that he sees the cause of his failures as external, whereas it is in fact within his own nature. This motif is repeated in the *Patna* episode, when he can see nothing but the fact of the 'chance missed'. The second crisis is the voyage out to the East, where he is first disabled by a falling spar, and thereafter the slow process of degeneration begins. In the slow, idyllic world of the East and of the *Patna* the illusion of peace 'the eternal peace of the Eastern seas' blends with his own dream-making to lull him into inaction, so that when the crisis of the accident comes, he is left doing nothing, not so much as the whining engineer with the broken arm. In the boat his dramatic but inactive pose stresses the isolation of the man both from his fellow-creatures and from reality. To both he is brought back through the trial and the interview with Marlow; at the former, he is made to answer 'questions so much to the point' (which to him are 'so useless') and is condemned for 'utter disregard of [his] plain duty'—in his conversations with Marlow, he is brought back out of his unreal world:

> With every instant he was penetrating deeper into the impossible world of romantic achievements. He had got to the heart of it at last! A strange look of beatitude overspread his features, his eyes sparkled in the light of the candle burning between us; he positively smiled! . . . I whisked him back by saying, 'If you had stuck to the ship, you mean!' He turned . . . as though he had tumbled down from a star.                    (vii.)

He roams around in the succession of unsatisfactory jobs, in the fallow period of the book, waiting for the chance to come again. He is given the chance by the fellow-romantic Stein, who in the central chapter of the book (both formally and thematically) defines Jim as nearly as he can be defined in words. The story of Jim's adventures in Patusan corresponds with the first part in a parallel movement. For example, the boat-trip up the river, with Jim squatting in the stern with the empty revolver in his hand parallels the scene after the accident to the *Patna*, where he had sat in the bow brandishing silently his piece of wood. Here it is his activity, stirring up the lethargic, passive natives, that achieves results. He is tireless in the regulation of things. He is now set up as the magistrate, going miles to settle a feud over three brass pots. He follows Stein in his actions, beating off his intended assassins and thereby winning his woman. He seems, in fact, to have conquered that 'place of decay' which made him of 'sound principle' but 'subtle unsoundness' (viii.) At this point, however, comes the reversal, the irony of the novel, For at the end Jim is as it were overtaken by a malignant Fate, in that the meeting with Brown is something for which one could not be prepared, something which could not have been expected, as he has tried to persuade himself and others was the case with his former actions and failures. His reasonable reactions to the matter of Brown are overreached by the unexpected treachery of Brown; but then the old Jim returns, as he goes to Doramin and permits himself to be shot. This, as we shall suggest later, is as much a failure in its way, and directed by the same personal romanticism, as were the earlier failures.

Thus we have in the main structure two versions, as it

were, of the life of the same man, except that the second is overshadowed and limited to some extent by the life of the first. What is to be our judgement on these lives? Are we to say that the first offers the life of a failure, the second a successful life (successful spiritually, if tragic physically) —or are we to say that the fact that they are the life of the same man means that, whatever the circumstances, the outcome will be the same? The structure leaves this to us. We can see the structure as a fall and a rising again, if we will; or we can see it as neutral, as two parallel lines inviting comparison. For comparison, mainly tacit, is the technique by which Conrad achieves many of his effects and upon which he bases his judgements, expressed or implied. Indeed, this may well be called the basic principle of his structural and narrative practice: the construction of situations in which the characters may be seen performing comparable actions, in order that we may form a judgement. Thus Jim's career in Patusan parallels that of Stein in Celebes; and the action of the French lieutenant who remained thirty hours on the *Patna*, of the native helmsmen who stuck to the wheel, and of Bob Stanton who was drowned saving a lady's maid because he would not jump, all bear upon Jim's jump from the *Patna*. We shall continually notice examples of this kind of technique throughout the novel; in such wise, in fact, that we shall, I think, see that what we have to do with here is not so much a broken-backed novel as rather one that may be thought to be too highly-wrought.

## Conrad's Narrative Technique

Conrad's technique of narration here as in so many of his novels is complex in the extreme. We open the novel with a sight of Jim in his capacity as water-clerk; that is to say, after he has the *Patna* incident and Marlow's attempts at rehabilitation behind him. We hear of his being driven further Eastwards by some as yet undefined and unmotivated impulse. Then we return to his early history, to the episode of the training-ship, the episode of the 'missed chance' of the rescue. Jim's views of this are given, and his contempt for the boy who had actually performed the rescue is shewn. We also see his naïve belief in himself, and in the capacity which he thinks himself to have to improve more by not having taken part than the actual rescuer:

> Otherwise he was rather glad he had not gone into the cutter, since a lower achievement had served the turn. He had enlarged his knowledge more than those who had done the work. (i.)

Thus we are introduced to one of his characteristics, that of perpetually placing potentiality above action. He will repeat this attitude to Marlow after the *Patna* incident, first unconsciously, when he retreats into his beatific vision-world, and later when he claims to be ready for anything: 'If this business couldn't knock me over, then there's no fear of there not being enough time to — climb out, and . . .' (xvi.) He shows this attitude in many other places.

We hear in the next chapter of his early experiences at sea, of his disablement in the fierce storm, at the beginning of the week, before he has had the opportunity to come into action—he is 'secretly rather glad that he had not to go on deck'. When they arrive at Singapore, he enters the hospital, and afterwards joins the loungers: the Eastern languor is well described, the enchantment of idleness and its effects, which we have already seen operative in both characters of sailors which Conrad distinguishes in the harbour. These characteristics we feel to be present, actually or potentially, in Jim. The disdain for these men overcome, he joins the *Patna*, and we are shown the ship, the captain and the pilgrims. The voyage begun, Conrad shows us the stillness, peace and unreality of these Eastern seas. Whilst Jim is on watch, there are flashes in which we glimpse the pilgrims, the Arab who is their leader, and the chartroom. The flow of Jim's thoughts is interrupted by the crash of the bucket, restoring in a pathetic way the reality to this dream world so reminiscent of the state of the Ancient Mariner's vessel. The characters of Jim's fellow officers are shown, partly narrated, partly coming through their speeches. The whine of the second engineer's plaints leads up to the collision, which is narrated indirectly: the drunken engineer first falls, with an oath, so that at first we think it to be from drink: then Jim and the captain stagger, 'and, catching themselves up, stood very stiff and still gazing, amazed at the undisturbed level of the sea. Then they looked upwards at the stars.'

The question, 'What had happened'? is not directly answered—rather we have an insight into the thoughts which overcome the crew when the suspicion of some undefined evil is raised. Mention is made of the sound, as of thunder; then only at the last of the feelings:

> The sharp hull driving on its way seemed to rise a few inches in succession through its whole length, as though it had become pliable, and settled down again rigidly to its work . . . (iii.)

Still we do not know what has happened, still less are we aware of all that is to come. The accident is related 'as though the ship had steamed across a narrow belt of vibrating water and of humming air'. (iii). Straightway we move to the courtroom, where, a month later, we see Jim giving evidence. We hear Conrad's reflections on the evidence, yet we still do not know of Jim's disgraceful behaviour during the accident. Marlow is introduced, as an observer—a significant introduction to what is to be his role in the novel as a whole—Jim meets his eyes, and the scene is set for Marlow's narration. Yet the central fact is still withheld from us, the fact of Jim's having jumped. What, then, is the purpose of these first four chapters?

In a roundabout method, we are made acquainted with most (though not all) of the facts of Jim's case, of the elements which are to be discussed in this first part of the book. We learn also of the early experiences, of Jim's thoughts and the like, which Marlow could not be expected to know and which Jim would not readily tell him, and which it would thus be improper for him to relate. (How concerned Conrad was with the appearance of truth in this matter is shown by his remarks in the preface concerning the length required for the narration.) Secondly, the 'omniscient author's' opening gives us a certain amount of factual, objective authority on which to base our judgement of the interpretations provided through the speeches, direct and indirect, supplied by Jim, Marlow, Brierly, the Court and other characters.

Conrad's technique of ignoring chronology and also of concentrating upon the apparently trivial or irrelevant as an index of significance is well shown in the next passage, where Marlow opens his long narrative. He plunges as it were *in medias res*, just as the opening of the novel itself did:

'Oh, yes, I attended the inquiry,' he would say, 'and to
this day I haven't left off wondering why I went. I am
willing to believe each of us has a guardian angel, if you
fellows will concede that each of us has a familiar devil
as well . . . He is there, right enough, and, being
malicious, he lets me in for that kind of thing. What
kind of thing, you ask? Why, the inquiry thing, the
yellow dog thing—you wouldn't think a mangy,
native tyke would be allowed to trip up people in the
veranda of a magistrate's court, would you? . . . &c.'

(v.)

Here several things are being done at once. Our interest is
caught by the immediacy of the words, by the urgency of
the utterance, and by the elliptical mode of the puzzled
speech of Marlow. Themes are introduced—the notion of
the incubus or familiar devil, which for its own malign
ends pursues us independently of our will in any matter—
continuity of incident is provided by the reference to the
inquiry upon which we had entered in the last chapter—
and incident and theme are combined in the enigmatic and
for several chapters totally unexplained episode of the
yellow dog, the cur of cowardice. This dog, it will be
remembered, is the occasion of Jim's first self-revelation
to Marlow, the involuntary acknowledgement of guilt
which is made by the mistake over the referend of Marlow's friend's words, 'Look at that cur'. So the enigma
prepares us by its intrinsic interest to give the incident
when it is finally explained our full attention.

As an introduction, then, it has the good qualities of
gripping attention and proposing themes. It should not be
forgotten, however, that it is in fact a second opening, and
there must be a slight feeling of disappointment on the

part of the reader that we have apparently made a false start at the beginning of the book. This is, perhaps, the disadvantage, on a first reading, of the disjointed and non-chronological method of narration which Conrad adopts, namely that the reader, losing his bearings, is likely to lose his patience as well.

What, then, are the advantages of this technique? It is manifest that it is used throughout the novel, and we need not trouble to demonstrate it in such detail further. In part, the confusion of chronology is doubtless part of the general confusion of the accepted which is a theme in the novel, part of the general departure from normality which is a feature of Jim's character. Furthermore, it is useful as a technique of suspense, as we build up, say, through a gradual revelation to the fact of Jim's jumping and then to his admission of it. Sometimes, by providing us with the inkling of a conclusion, it may serve to redirect our suspense and attention away from the obvious features, such as the bare facts, towards the meaning or towards the manner of an incident. Such, for example, is the purpose served by the hints given at the beginning of Marlow's report, where Gentleman Brown is introduced in his decrepit triumph. This instils into us a sense of fearful expectation; we know or guess that something terrible has happened to Jim through Brown, and our attention is directed on to the means by which these two were brought together and on to the manner of Brown's triumph. In the end, we find that the triumph was accomplished by a most curious chain of circumstances, requiring for its performance as a pre-condition the peculiar natures of the actors in the Patusan drama.

Or, again, the technique can serve to impart immediacy within a framework of report after the event, as when for example we have the technique of 'flashback' used whilst Jim is relating his story to Marlow at the Malabar Hotel. Starting from this firm base of reality we move into the unreal world of the *Patna* and Jim; yet at the back of our minds we have always the familiar reality of the hotel, of the tourists, our like, who surround the two; and behind that, too, the company at Charley's, to which we are brought back frequently, by a passing reference ('Charley here knew him well . . .'; 'Some of you fellows must have known . . .') or by the complete stopping of the story, as in Chapter VIII, where Marlow, brooding on the significance of this 'lost youngster, one in a million—but then he was one of us' wonders whether 'the obscure truth involved were momentous enough to affect mankind's conception of itself'. At this point, before we launch on to the uncharted seas of metaphysical speculation, Conrad brings us back to a sense of everyday normality through the detail of Marlow's stopping to light his cigar. Likewise with Jim's confessions at the Malabar Hotel. From time to time we are brought back to the Malabar, and it is worth noticing how deftly Conrad can do this: after Marlow's digression on the French lieutenant, we have a sight of Jim at De Jongh's, we are told the tale of Bob Stanton ('Charley here knew him well'—a neat touch to remind us of Marlow's audience) and then back through a reminiscence of Marlow's, from the point of view of the moment when he had been talking to the French lieutenant, of the time when Jim had come to see him after the trial (we have not yet had this incident narrated regularly) through a reflection on Brierly's offer, back to the veranda of the Malabar, where Jim had been telling his tale. The modulation is perfect. There is no sudden cut; rather, to use the language of the films, a gradual fade-out of the digression and a fade-in of the scene at the Malabar. The technique here serves to span wide and differing scenes, and to draw together in one moment several scenes which are thematically but not narratively related. Thus we have the comparison of the Bob Stanton episode invoked in express connection with Jim's views on himself; and we have a reminder of Brierly's views and Brierly's offer, and thus of Brierly himself and the comparison which was made between Brierly and Jim.

In later chapters the same technique is used, the same pattern is found. Conrad cuts back and forth among his various stages, and sees those at various times. Subordinate characters such as the Dutch colonial official and the scribe are brought in to give evidence as to the fame of Jim. Brown's narrative is pieced together by Marlow after we have already seen the dying Brown. The audience changes, and narrows from the after-dinner gathering to the solitary 'privileged man'; an indication, perhaps, of the increasing isolation of Jim.

One is left at the latter end with an overpowering sense of Jim's loneliness. In part this is self-inflicted, as when after the episode in the training ship he broods apart, or when on the *Patna* he thinks of himself as separate from the other members of the crew. His distinction of himself is at first a self-laudatory, afterwards a self-condemnatory one, and each time unnecessary. In each case he cuts himself off from the world and from the society around him, considering himself a being apart; whereas he is in fact 'one of us'. The result of this is that he is eventually expelled by the world around him. Brierly thinks that the best thing he could do would be to crawl into a hole twenty feet underground and stay there. (vi.) Egstrøm thinks that the world will not be big enough to hold his caper. (xviii.) Marlow says that there is no fear that the door will not be slammed firmly shut behind him. (xxii.) He comes himself to see what the optimistic Marlow does not—that even in Patusan he is 'not good enough' for the outside world.

Jim first introduces the phrase 'not good enough' during his conversation with Marlow at the Malabar Hotel, and thereafter refers to it throughout the book. Marlow is concerned to show him, on the one hand, that it is only Jim's own stupidity which prevents him from returning—for Marlow sees the rehabilitation process in Patusan as making Jim eventually fit to return—and he says that it is only Jim's curious sort of personal pride that prevents his return. Yet, on the other hand, Marlow too recognizes, for all his apparent agreement with Egstrøm's 'And who the devil cares about that?', that there is a sense in which Jim, by his jump, has plunged into an 'everlasting deep hole'. The isolation which he has thereby brought upon himself is not, as in his more optimistic moments Marlow thinks it to be, temporary. Jim has isolated himself effectively from the world by his jump; at once from the sordid elements, in separating himself both in the boat and on the wharf from the captain and the engineers, and also from the society of men such as his father wishes him to be among. In the end Jim comes to exist for himself alone apart from any other being; separated from his family by his own act which has put him outside their morality and therefore has for ever separated him from them; separated from Jewel, whom he never really understands as a woman, as, indeed, other than a precious toy. He regards her as something precious, something which he has been lucky to find, indeed, as lucky as if he had discovered the emerald which the scribe and the Dutch colonial official think him to have found: but something, nevertheless, which he is not prepared to regard as fully human in any real sense.

So he abandons her, separating himself wantonly from her, and dies in the end abandoned by all—isolated from his own race, and surrounded by those who do not understand him and what he stands for. Marlow's last glimpse of him is as a supremely isolated figure:

> Their dark-skinned bodies vanished on the dark background long before I had lost sight of their protector. He was white from head to foot, and remained persistently visible with the stronghold of the night at his back, the sea at his feet, the opportunity by his side—still veiled. What do you say? Was it still veiled? I don't know. For me, that whole figure in the stillness of coast and sea seemed to stand at the heart of a vast enigma. The twilight was ebbing fast from the sky above his head, the strip of sand had sunk already under his feet, he himself appeared no bigger than a child—then only a speck, a tiny white speck, that seemed to catch all the light left in a darkened world . . . and, suddenly, I lost him . . . (xxxv.)

*Questions and Projects:*

1. Write an essay in which you try to recapture your feelings and critical reactions on first reading *Lord Jim*.

2. What justification do you find for Conrad's unusual method of narration in *Lord Jim*?

3. What, if anything, do you think *Lord Jim* would have lost, had Conrad dispensed with Marlow and written the story of Jim as a straight-forward narrative?

4. Collect instances from *Lord Jim* where Conrad employs devices that we usually associate with the technique of the film or television.

5. Make a list of examples of the following features that are clearly marked in *Lord Jim*:

(a) Repetition or parallel use of incidents or phrases. (In each instance add a note on what function is served thereby.)

(b) References to imagination or to the imaginative element in the character of Jim.

(c) Instances of Jim's behaviour which are morally ambiguous.

6. Make a study (in note form) of one or two other novels (e.g. by Virginia Woolf) where an unusual narrative technique is used: add notes to show what effect or purpose is served thereby.

## 3. POINT OF VIEW; THE USE OF THE MINOR CHARACTERS

We have spoken of Conrad's 'judgement' as though there were some simple answer to this novel, some single lesson taught by it. Nevertheless, Marlow spends the whole of what is in any comparison a long novel in attempting to get to the depths of Jim, and finding himself constantly thrown back. There are moments, indeed, when he begins to doubt the possibility of plumbing Jim's depths—and other moments when he doubts the very existence of those depths. Jim rejects Marlow's offer of help,

> holding fast to some deep idea which I could detect shimmering like a pool of water in the dark, but which I despaired of ever approaching near enough to fathom . . . 'I am able to help what I can see of you. I don't pretend to do more.' . . . 'You are too superficial', I said (and at the same time I was thinking to myself: 'Well, here goes! and perhaps he is after all.')
> (xvii.)

Some critics have indeed felt that Conrad is making a great pother about nothing, or that in talking so much around the subject he is merely demonstrating that he himself has not a very clear notion of what he wants to say. Marlow's fumbling, Mr. Stewart considers, is indicative of Conrad's own woolly-mindedness about the matter. This may well be our conclusion after having read the book, and it may be that this is one of the principal causes of the dissatisfaction that is felt with the novel by many readers. There is, perhaps, a sense in which Jim's affair is both deep and superficial, in that we cannot, in the last resort, any more than the Court could, identify the ultimate *Why?* The heart of the great mystery at which Jim stands is this inability to do more than define areas of contributory causes (egoism, indecision and the like) whereas the reason why Jim should be possessed by such demons is inexplicable. We cannot say why the appearance should deceive, why the sovereign should turn out to be nothing more rare than brass. It is not possible to identify the place of decay. In this sense Jim remains deep, we have lost him. But the fact that we can say as much as we have of his character indicates that there is also a certain super-ficiality about him, that there is much which only appears to be complex. Once we recognize the centrality of his own self to Jim, he is explicable—our doubts are perhaps more of the validity of the terms we use to describe him.

Conrad uses many devices in his investigation of Jim: direct comment; simple presentation of Jim in certain situations, with the reader left to draw the necessary inferences from the facts; he uses Marlow's cogitations; above all, perhaps, he uses contact with other characters and their points of view. Point of view is always impor-tant in Conrad's technique, and in *Heart of Darkness*, for example, we can see how the points of view narrow down in decreasing cones on to the figure of Kurtz. But *Lord Jim* is even more a novel of opinions, of points of view. Marlow 'was always eager to take opinion on it, as though it had not been practically settled: individual opinion— international opinion . . .' (xiv.). The various opinions are used to give insight and to pass judgement. Sometimes,

as in the case of Marlow's audience, to whom we are
constantly brought back, the judgement is unexpressed,
reserved; their function is to present a certain sort of
attitude which is at once more immediate, as being one
step nearer than ourselves to the story, and more limited,
as being conditioned, for example by their knowledge of
Marlow and their attitude to him; by their Philistine
attitudes; and limited too by their lack of knowledge. The
'privileged man' who reads the final reports from Marlow
knows more, but here again he is but an attitude to the
tale rather than a commentator upon it. What is to be said,
then, of these silent figures? Their attitudes point the way
for our own. Conrad protests against regarding the tale as
a yarn merely, in Marlow's early words:

> Charley, my dear chap, your dinner was extremely good,
> and in consequence these men here took upon a quiet
> rubber as a tumultuous occupation. They wallow in
> your good chairs and think to themselves, 'Hang
> exertion. Let that Marlow talk'.                    (v.)

Marlow protests further against the prosaic view of Jim
in his words which serve to recall the audience and to
indicate their probable attitude, when he speaks of 'an
utterly uninteresting bit of business—what Charley here
would call one of my rational transactions'. (xiii.) The
attitude taken up by Charley and the others present at the
dinner is one of indifference, attention to the story for its
narrative value rather than for its meaning, and, perhaps, a
certain readiness to accept the obvious in interpretation of
Jim's actions. (Cf. Charley's protest, 'You are so subtle,
Marlow.') The 'privileged man,' on the other hand, adopts
the attitude of interested study of the facts as they are
presented to him by Marlow.

c

Marlow's own point of view, whilst present throughout, is somewhat nebulous and uncertain. His principal function is a combination of the showman, bringing on various 'turns' for our entertainment (as Thackeray in *Vanity Fair* or Alban Berg in *Lulu* do more overtly) and the somewhat fumbling reasoner. He thinks as he speaks, and has definite points of view to put forward about the criteria by which Jim is to be judged, but he does not seem to provide anything particularly valuable in the way of insight. The insight is mostly provided in flashes by the minor characters, by a word from Jones, or Brierly, or Egstrøm, or Chester. An example of Marlovian cogitation is this:

> For my part, I cannot say what I believed—indeed, I don't know to this day, and never shall probably. But what did the poor devil believe himself? Truth shall prevail—don't you know *Magna est veritas et* . . . Yes, when it gets a chance. There is a law, no doubt—and likewise a law regulates your luck in the throwing of the dice. It is not Justice the servant of men, but accident, hazard. Fortune—the ally of patient Time—that holds an even and scrupulous balance. Both of us had said the very same thing. Did we both speak the truth— or did one of us—or neither?                    (xxxiv.)

This is a very confused set of phrases. It does not, indeed, sound like the efforts of a man to come to a decision or even struggling to express himself, to find the right words, but rather like a man who has no real comprehension of the matter, who is fumbling for something to say because he does not understand—some would say, neither does Conrad.

For a part of the book, that dealing with Jim in Patusan,

the phrase 'one of us' which we have examined is laid aside; perhaps because this part is no longer so much under the control of Marlow, as the representative of the craft of the sea, but rather under the aegis of Stein. The transition is effected in such a way as to maintain the idea of Jim's universal significance and relevance which has been raised by 'one of us'—in Marlow's visit to Stein to discuss Jim. Here we have presented the point of view of Stein, which illuminates the whole of the subsequent part of the work in the same way that Marlow's views had dominated the first part. Marlow introduces the subject of Jim to Stein by saying that he has brought a specimen, not a butterfly, but a man. 'Well,' says Stein, 'I am a man, too.' (xx.) Stein's words introduce us to the role which he has in the point of view technique, the maintenance of the role of man seeking that part of himself, the truth about himself, which is to be found in Jim. Marlow sees him as the medical expert, invested with all the objectivity and authority which attend that office:

> He had diagnosed the case for me, and at first I was quite startled to find how simple it was; and indeed our conference resembled so much a medical consultation —Stein, of learned aspect, sitting in an armchair before his desk; I, anxious, in another, facing him, but a little to one side—that it seemed natural to ask, 'What's good for it?' (xx.)

Stein's point of view in the case is that of the detached observer, the scientific expert, who is involved in the matter by virtue of his being in the line which hands on, as Marlow puts it to Jim, the experience and the knowledge of what has gone before it. He is seen to be the heir to the tradition established by the Scotsman and handed on to him, and which he now passes on to Jim. In this way Jim, rejected by one tradition whose code he has betrayed, the sea, enters, through the human kindness of Stein, into another within which he may again find this place in society. Although he cannot return—a fact which he recognizes and which Marlow acknowledges—by virtue of his failure in the matter of the *Patna* (as Stein, by his political activities, made himself socially unacceptable in Bavaria) still he may find rehabilitation within a different context, a context divorced from home, but one which offers possibilities both within the immediate colonial context and in continued, if posthumous, contact with Europe (as Stein has built up his reputation as an entomologist, and intends to leave his collection to his native village). In fact, as the example of Stein shows, the work performed in the East may well lead to the reacceptance of the exile in his homeland, even if only after his death, as is figured in the fact that Stein is going to leave his collection to the village of his birth, thus at the same time effecting a reconciliation with those who rejected him (or whom he rejected) and giving them a tangible proof of his prowess and worthiness to be thus reaccepted. Stein rejected in his youth the society of Bavaria, and left to seek the gratification of a kind of romantic ideal in much the same way as Jim (although Jim's impulse was forced on much slenderer grounds: '. . . after a course of light holiday literature his vocation for the sea had declared itself . . .' (i.)) His own tendency towards romanticism is shown by his being a revolutionary of the '48, and in his subsequent career in Celebes, a country which 'can scarcely be said to have an interior'. (xx.). In the same way as Jim, he is one talked about—his defence of the Scotsman's enclosure with twenty natives against an army is still mentioned with respect. Like Jim, he is attached to the native rulers, to Mohammed Bonso and to the princess, as Jim to Doramin and his family; like Jim, he brings about the discomfiture of his ambushers. So much connection with the history of Jim cannot but invite comparison; and the fact that Stein himself is placed in the context of a tradition, placed so emphatically as to be accounted by the Scotsman, 'my son', is important in evaluating how Jim stands up to the new demands of this new tradition—a tradition which he recognizes as such: he realizes that he is being made the custodian of the responsibilities of Stein towards Doramin and Patusan. And his interpretation, as we have said, turns out to be insufficient.

To return to Stein's romanticism: there is, besides these factual pointers (the exchange of the ring; the use of the sentimentally evocative term 'war-comrade' for Doramin —a term which in the German, *Kriegskamerad*, is both more common and more sentimental than the English equivalent—indeed, Jim fails to understand the full force of the word for Stein, and considers it 'funny')—there is the evidence of Stein's words. These express an underlying Romanticism which has, however, in his case found disciplined expression in the scientific pursuit of entomology: the regularization or ascertainment of the ephemeral, the beautiful, the romantic in scientific forms; the imposition of order upon the wildness of nature, the capturing and subduing to man's will of beauty and transience. He speaks, more than does Jim, of dreams; but where Jim languishes and loses himself in them as purposeful:

'To follow the dream, and again to follow the dream— and so—ewig—usque ad finem.' (xx.)

Stein gives us here a glimpse of that Romantic *Sehnsucht nach der Ewigkeit* which is not enervating, but inspirational, and that because there is an end to it. For all the characters in this novel, at least, the end is one of tragedy, not of fulfilment—or if of fulfilment, of a very equivocal nature —of Jim gone to his 'pitiless wedding', of Jewel and Stein, the precious things of the earth, leading a 'soundless, inert life . . . preparing to leave'. Is this, then, the end of the Romantic Dream?

In Patusan, Stein's counterpart, by the relation hinted at between them, as also by the chosen nomenclature, is Jewel. ('Jewel' is one of the meanings of Stein.) She is yet another aspect of Jim's responsibility towards his kind, this time seen in terms of personal loyalty. In jumping from the *Patna* he had betrayed a communal code; in going deliberately to his 'pitiless wedding with a shadowy code of conduct' he is betraying a human being, as well as the collective humanity of the settlement. This betrayal is well conveyed in sexual terms—the image of opportunity as the 'veiled Eastern bride' which is used by Marlow several times both before and after his knowledge of Jim's end, sets off the suggestion of the kind of 'betrayal' of which Jewel's mother was the victim—her lover, too, abandoned her, went, 'out there', as Jewel says, using 'out there' in the sense of all those moral imperatives which she does not comprehend and which, within the microcosm of Patusan, do not exist—those abstract and bodiless moralities which form the door slammed to behind Jim, that stand between him and his kind. In Jewel, he finds no luxurious connection, but rather the austere fulfilment of a part of his task and an inspiration by the way—but in the last resort, he does not need her and he abandons her to her fate. The importance of human relationship, and the

tragedy which results from its being ignored or discounted
in favour of some other thing, ideal or concrete, is here
shewn and made a part of the universal message by being
placed, again, in the context of tradition. As it was to
Jewel's mother, so to Jewel. There is throughout the work
a sense of the changelessness of the human lot, expressed
in the form, now of tradition, now of repetition. In each
generation certain characters are the same, certain actions
are repeated: there is always a woman whose life is sacrificed by her lover for the sake of 'out there'.

One of the principal methods of universalizing the
meaning of Jim is to set him in situations where he is
compared and contrasted with others who are expressions
of his own characteristics writ large, made gross, carried to
their ultimate end. Thus Brown and Chester may be seen as
exaggerations of the same traits in Jim, and in such of his
kind as were seen at the beginning on Singapore harbour:

> These were of two kinds. Some, very few and seen
> there but seldom, led mysterious lives, had preserved
> an undefaced energy with the temper of buccaneers, the
> eyes of dreamers. They appeared to live in a crazy maze
> of plans, hopes, dangers, enterprises, ahead of civili-
> zation, in the dark places of the sea; and their death was
> the only event of their fantastic existence that seemed
> to have a reasonable certitude of achievement. The
> majority were men who, like himself, thrown there by
> some accident, had remained as officers of country
> ships. They had now a horror of the home service, with
> its harder conditions, severer view of duty, and the
> hazard of stormy oceans. They were attuned to the
> eternal peace of Eastern sky and sea . . . They shud-
> dered at the thought of hard work, and led precariously

> easy lives, always on the verge of dismissal, always on
> the verge of engagement, serving Chinamen, Arabs,
> half-castes—would have served the Devil himself had
> he made it easy enough . . . &c.                    (ii.)

Of the former kind, the examples in the book are pre-
eminently Chester and Brown. The curious episode of
Chester and Captain Robinson seems to be brought in for
the purpose of showing this kind of character at one
extreme of its possible development, as Brown shows it
at another, and as Stein shows it drawn to an apparently
successful conclusion. Chester and the half-crazed Captain
Robinson, known as Holy-Terror Robinson in the days
before decrepitude had set in to mock him, exist in this
world of schemes and adventures which never come to
anything; and their death is a thing as uncertain as their
life. Information comes that they are missing, that a wreck
has been sighted, but nothing is known for certain. Yet
their plans, if crazy, were at least active and purposeful,
and even after Jim has gone to Patusan Marlow wonders
from time to time whether it might not have been better
to have closed with Chester's 'confoundedly generous
offer'. Chester and Robinson may be comic characters,
pitiful in some respects, but not contemptible. Conrad has
still a respect for their adventurousness, for their readiness to go anywhere, in the most ramshackle vessels; for
their unwillingness to give up. He reserves his contempt for
those whose schemes are conceived from the point of
view of the middleman, such as that one whom Marlow
meets, as he is going to meet Jim, 'a fellow fresh from
Madagascar with a wonderful piece of business. It had
something to do with cattle and cartridges and a Prince
Ravonalo something; but the pivot of the whole affair

was the stupidity of some admiral—Admiral Pierre, I think. Everything turned on that, and the chap couldn't find words strong enough to express his confidence. He had globular eyes starting out of his head with a fishy glitter, bumps on his forehead, and wore his long hair brushed back without a parting. He had a favourite phrase which he kept repeating triumphantly, "The minimum of risk with the maximum of profit is my motto. What?" '

Chester and Robinson, on the other hand, if 'a curious pair of Argonauts' are still treated with the respect for the adventurer which that word conveys. They, and their episode, to which allusion is made constantly afterwards, have been seen as irrelevant, as spoiling the shape of the narrative. Nevertheless, none of the minor characters is irrelevant in this novel: each has something to offer in the way of shedding light on Jim, whether directly, by contact with him, or, as here, indirectly, by expressing characteristics of Jim in another context. What Chester and Robinson (and Brown, in another way) are doing is to offer as it were an alternative ending to the story of Jim; given these and these circumstances, this, and not Patusan, would have been the story of Jim. A modern writer such as Brecht may venture to offer us the same story told about the same characters with a different ending to make his point (Cp. *Der Ja-sager und der Nein-Sager*)[1] whereas the more conventional method is to present similar characters in extreme positions.

If Chester represents one possible evolution of that first kind of seamen described in the passage quoted about those in Singapore harbour, Brown represents another, and therewith another possible ending for the Jim story—

---

[1] *He Who Said Yes and He Who Said No* (Berlin 1930. English Trans. 1946).

the pirate. Here too there is respect; an unwilling respect extorted by the fearsome achievements of the man. We have mentioned the lack of respect for humanity which makes him a figure comparable with Jim; we may note, too, that there are other points of contact. Like Jim and Stein, he is placed in the situation of defending a narrow place against odds; and the effect of the comparison is to show that the same quality of character may operate on either side of the fence. 'Change places, and, handy-dandy, which is the justice, which is the thief?' The daring acts are there, only this time in the service of crime instead of justice: and the callous Brown who leaves his man dying by the boat shews essentially the same trait that causes Jim to abandon Jewel. To this type of nature, Conrad is saying, the rightness of the cause in the eyes of the world is immaterial, for it despises the world in its own egoism.

Not in Chester and Brown alone do we find the sort of extreme statement of what Jim is, or might be—we find a hint of the same thing in the gun-runner; even, in the disgusting hulk of the New South Wales German, the captain of the *Patna*. Here too is a despiser of standards:

'You damned Englishmen can do your worst; I know where there's plenty room for a man like me: I am well aguaindt in Apia, in Honolulu, in . . . What are you to shout? Eh? You tell me? You are no better than other people, and that old rogue he make Gottam fuss with me.' (v.)

At bottom, this is no more than a crude expression of the same sort of feeling that causes Jim to ask of Marlow, 'Don't you sometimes think yourself a—a—cur?' The feeling that rejects the simple uprightness of a man like Captain Elliot, or the outspokenness of a man like Captain

O'Brien—what is there to choose? This is the function of
these minor characters—to set off Jim's words by putting
them into bolder, cruder practice, and thereby shewing
the true nature of the poses which Jim takes up. They are
the antidote to the insidious arguments which sway
Marlow; they show us what we must expect if we accept
the arguments which Jim puts forward. Marlow, Elliot,
O'Brien, Jones, Jim's father are all bound by their code of
behaviour which knows what is right: with Chester,
Brown and Jim, distinctions are blurred by casuistry.

> 'It was not a lie—but it wasn't truth all the same.
> It was something . . . ? One knows a downright lie.
> There was not the thickness of a sheet of paper between
> the right and wrong of this affair.'
> —'How much more did you want?' I asked . . .
> . . . 'A hair's breadth,' he muttered. 'Not the breadth
> of a hair between this and that. And at the time . . .'
> —'It is difficult to see a hair at midnight,' I put in, a
> little viciously, I fear. Don't you see what I mean by the
> solidarity of the craft?'                              (xi.)

*Images of Corruption*

The second type of sailor to be found in the harbour of
Singapore (*vid. sup.*) is contrasted with these adventurers.
These are the 'loungers through existence'. In all there is
the 'soft spot, the place of decay'. The foremost representative in the book is probably Cornelius; but other minor
figures representing this type are found—as, for example,
the Dutch colonial official:

> . . . a third-class deputy-assistant resident, a big, fat,
> greasy, blinking fellow of mixed descent, with turned-
> out, shiny lips. I found him lying extended on his back

in a cane chair, odiously unbuttoned, with a large green
leaf of some sort on the top of his steaming head, and
another in his hand which he used lazily as a fan . . .
                                                    (xxviii.)

This figure represents the extreme of decay. He is almost
physically decomposing as we see him. The image of
corruption and decay is a pervasive one in this book, and
we find it associated always with this type of character. It
also provides another instance of the divergence of
appearance and reality, as we see the beginnings of decay
in Jim. From the outset Marlow says that 'he had no
business to look so sound'. (v.) The contrasting images of
the sound appearance and the inward corruption are
insisted upon throughout in regard to Jim. At that first
sight, Marlow considers that Jim is

the kind of fellow you would, on the strength of his
looks, leave in charge of the deck . . . I tell you I
ought to know the right kind of looks. I would have
trusted the deck to that youngster on the strength of a
single glance, and gone to sleep with both eyes—and
by Jove! it wouldn't have been safe.            (v.)

Marlow's view is that Jim's character, promising of so
sterling worth, is alloyed—that there is 'the least drop of
something rare, accursed' which makes one wonder
'whether perchance he were nothing more rare than
brass'. This image of the alloy is associated with another,
that of the 'soft-spot', the plague-spot, the place of decay.
This is something feared, something to be shunned even
more than the evident evil of someone like, say, the
German captain of the *Patna*, on whom the plague is
evident:

. . . he seemed to be swollen to an unnatural size by some awful disease, by the mysterious action of some unknown poison. (v.)

—or the corrupt Mariani or the shifty Schomberg. It is feared precisely because the disease is not evident. In the seamen of Singapore with whom Jim associates after leaving hospital, the disease is plain:

. . . in all they said—in their actions, in their looks, in their persons—could be detected the soft spot, the place of decay, the determination to lounge safely through existence.' (ii.)

Such characters are the engineers of the *Patna*, or the Danish officer of the King of Siam. When Jim, therefore, is gradually won over to them, when:

In time, beside the original disdain there grew up slowly another sentiment, and suddenly, giving up the idea of going home, he took a berth as chief mate on the *Patna*. (ii.)

we are aware that the curious lack of decision and activity which has been shown in the training ship and on the outward bound vessel is becoming the main feature of Jim's life. He is sinking and placing himself on a level with these corrupt and decayed Europeans whose only concept of distinction is that of being white. He is retiring into the unreal and corrupted world which they inhabit, and which his imagination creates for him; and thereby, by partitioning off the imagined from the real, by mistaking the corrupt for the sound, he becomes a traitor to that which he ought to uphold.

The image of corruption may be traced throughout the

presentation of Jim: here we will remark only its end, in the final dissolution of Brown:

> He said all these things in profound gasps, staring at me with his yellow eyes out of a long, ravaged, brown face, he jerked his left arm; a pepper-and-salt matted beard hung almost into his lap; a dirty ragged blanket covered his legs. (xxxvii.)

> As he was telling me this he tried with a shaking hand to wipe the thin foam on his blue lips . . . His own eyes were starting out of their sockets. He fell back, clawing the air with skinny fingers, sat up again, bowed and hairy, glared at me sideways like some man-beast of folklore, with open mouth in his miserable and awful agony before he got his speech back after that fit.
> (xl.)

The image of physical corruption and decay for spiritual is of course common; it is found, for example, in Defoe's two works on the Great Plague of London, the *Journal of the Plague Year* and the *Plague for Soul and Body*. Towards the end of the nineteenth century it became a much-used image: thus, for example, in Camus' *La Peste*, in Zola's *Nana*, in Wilde's *Portrait of Dorian Grey*. Here it is used to depict the final stage of those characters in whom the 'soft spot' is to be found; again, to express what Jim might, under certain other circumstances, have become. Marlow fears Jim's degeneration:

> It struck me that it is from such as he that the great army of waifs and strays is recruited, the army that marches, down, down, into all the gutters of the earth. As soon as he left my room, the 'bit of shelter' as he called it, he would take his place in the ranks, and begin the journey towards the bottomless pit. (xvi.)

The earth is so small that I was afraid of, some day, being waylaid by a blear-eyed, swollen-faced, besmirched loafer, with no soles to his canvas shoes, and with a flutter of rags about the elbows, who, on the strength of old acquaintance, would ask for a loan of five dollars. You know the awful jaunty bearing of these scare-crows coming to you from a decent past, the rasping careless voice, the half-averted impudent glances— those meetings more trying to a man who believes in the solidarity of our lives than the sight of an impenitent deathbed to a priest. (xxi.)

This meeting which Marlow fears is set against that which he imagines with those whom he has trained to the service of the Red Rag, the cheery young mates who meet him at the dockyard gate with a hearty slap on the back and a 'Do you remember me, sir? Young So-and-so'. Again, the images are of health and disease: 'sunburnt young chief mate'; 'fresh deep voice'; 'heavy young hand'; 'cheery sea-puppy voice'; 'hearty'; (v.) contrasted with 'blear-eyed'; 'swollen-faced'; &c. (xxi.). The various degrees of health and disease, appearance of health and decay, are used in the novel to measure the inward and spiritual state of the characters, how far their constitutions have been undermined by the corrupting influence of the East. In this respect Jim is saved from the corruption which attends Cornelius, Brown or the Dutch officer: yet there remains this weakness which is not evident as it is with them; this alloy, this plague-spot, which makes him essentially unsound.

*Questions and Projects*

1. Write a study of the nature of Marlow and show how this is used to throw light on the way Jim is seen and judged by others as well as by Jim himself.

2. Show the importance of Stein in both the narrative and moral interest of *Lord Jim*.

3. Illustrate and discuss the function and value of the following minor characters: Gentleman Brown; the French Lieutenant; Jewel.

4. To what extent can Jim be considered to be a tragic hero?

5. Find in other novels examples of characters who have to bear the consequences of an initial error of behaviour.

6. Collect examples from *Lord Jim* of Conrad's awareness of and interest in characters who in some way lead lives that set them apart from ordinary humanity.

## 4. LANGUAGE AND STYLE

It is well known that Conrad learned English as a second foreign language, and indeed it has been held that he thought in French and translated his thought thence into English. The influence of French is from time to time visible in his style, not only in those cases where he uses a vocabulary heavily Romance in character, but also in the use of the French idiom, or in the French construction, as in the placing of adjectives, for example. The use of syntax is always more important than the use of vocabulary alone in determining to what extent a writer has been influenced by a foreign language in his works: for example, Milton's vocabulary is not excessively Latinate (he introduces fewer Latin words to the language than Shakespeare) but his syntax shows how much he thought in Latin terms; whereas Johnson, whose vocabulary is noticeably Latinate, uses predominantly English syntax. Thus from time to time we detect the French turn of phrase in Conrad's work, as in the following examples:

'For that they were so, makes no doubt to me; given the state of the ship, this was the deadliest possible description of accident that could happen.' (viii.)

For the rest, he lived solitary, but not misanthropic. (xx.)

I do not mean to imply that I figured to myself the spirit of the land uprising above the white cliffs of Dover . . . (xxi.)

Other examples could be collected. It is not, I think, an especially important element in Conrad's language: but we may note that it appears predominantly at those points where attempts are being made at analytic presentation of some aspect of character, and this may show that Conrad, when he was thinking in this analytic way, used the French with its habit of distinction in thought. We will mention this again in a moment.

Most of *Lord Jim* is cast in the form of direct speech. This is characteristically unformed, even broken: in any event, immediate in conveying ideas and impressions. Of great interest is the use to which Conrad, who has an ear for several languages, can put variations in the speech of his characters—can, in fine, convey tones of speech and meaning as well through broken English as standard, within which he shews a fine discrimination of tone. The half-formed words, the speech broken with passion, the foreigner's English bestrewn with odd foreign phrases and words, the painful attempts to define and re-define which the characters—and most of all, of course, Marlow —make, underline the insufficiency of language in describing the case of Jim.

Let us consider some of the uses to which Conrad puts broken speech. Sometimes it is used to great dramatic effect, as when the judgement of the Court is delivered:

He stared with parted lips, hanging upon the words of the man behind the desk. These came out into the stillness wafted on the wind made by the punkahs, and I, watching for their effect upon him, caught only fragments of official language . . . 'The Court . . . Gustav So-and-so master . . . native of Germany . . . James So-and-so . . . mate . . . certificates cancelled.' A silence

fell. The magistrate had dropped the paper, and leaning
sideways on the arm of his chair, began to talk with
Brierly easily.                                          (xiv.)

Here Conrad is doing several things. The effect conveyed
by the language reproduces as it were in words the waves
of sound wafted across by the punkahs, and at the same
time conveys the confused effect which they have on Jim.
Likewise the broken effect causes the weight of the
description to fall on the words of sentence, 'certificates
cancelled'. Not only this, but also the fact that official
language, at once familiar and formal, is used: Marlow
obviously expects his hearers to be acquainted with the
form of words used. Further, there is an appropriateness
in the fact that it is this official language which is used, for
the conventional nature of the condemnation stresses the
importance of the conventions which Jim has flouted.
Indeed, we may go further, and say that the language in its
formal character takes on the nature of ritual, and thus
heightens the solemnity of Jim's casting-out. This
solemnity is then contrasted with the effect which it has on
the Court: for the magistrate, this is another piece of
business done with, and he can talk easily with Brierly
whilst waiting for the next case, the native assault-and-
battery case, to come up. For him, Jim's affair is obscure,
transient. There is also irony in the use of the word 'easily'
in connection with Brierly, for we, the readers, already
know that Brierly has been holding 'silent enquiry into
his own case' in the course of the trial, and that for him
as for Jim this is a momentous occasion. The formality of
the expulsion of Jim contrasts curiously with the easy
way in which the world which has cast him out regards
him after the business is over. This is constantly to be

brought up in the course of the book: 'who the devil cares about that?' The contrast between the momentousness of the proceedings and the casual attitude of the world thereafter is brought out in the contrast between the silence which comes over the courtroom at the sentence and the easy talk which follows the dropping of the paper itself recalls Jim's words (Chapter xi.) 'There was not the thickness of a sheet of paper between the right and wrong of this affair.' Finally, the effect of the broken language enables Conrad to avoid naming Jim by surname, which is not unimportant.

At this crisis in the action, therefore, there is a detachment, which is conveyed in the language, as we stand back, as it were, to take stock of the situation to this point. The official language, wafted in gusts to our ears, gives the required air of formality and detachment, the freedom from personal involvement, which is required at this stage, after the spiritual exercises of the past few chapters, where everything has been charged with emotion and immediate sense-impression. For a moment, the hurly-burly of Conrad's Eastern world stands still, and there is a brief silence whilst we take stock of the importance of this moment.

From the fragments of official language we turn to another sort of fragmentary language, that of the half-caste captain on the vessel which takes Jim to Patusan.

His flowing English seemed to be derived from a dictionary compiled by a lunatic. Had Mr. Stein desired him to 'ascend', he would have 'reverentially' (I think he wanted to say respectfully—but devil only knows) 'reverentially made objects for the safety of properties' ... Mr. Cornelius 'propitiated many offertories' to Mr.

Rajah Allang and the 'principal populations' on condi-
tions which made the trade 'a snare and ashes in the
mouth' yet his ship had been fired on from the woods
by 'irresponsive parties' . . . the Rajah was a 'laughable
hyena' (can't imagine how he got hold of hyenas) . . .

(xxiii.)

The mixture noticeable here is of Marlow's amused contempt for the half-caste's solecisms (perhaps prompted by
the fashion in this sort of English set by such works as
*English as she is spoke*, the extracts of the best solecisms
from Pedro Carolino's Portuguese-English phrase book)
combined with a curious sort of prophetic wisdom in the
malapropisms. How well, for example, the word 'propitiated' suits the cringing Cornelius; and the ritual word
'offertories' for 'offerings' underlines the sort of sacrifice
which Jim is later to make to the veiled Eastern goddess
of his world of dreams. The religious connotations of
'offertories' react in turn upon 'propitiated' which thus
takes on a ritual sense (as in the First Epistle of John).
Here we see the force, perhaps, of 'reverentially'—the
passage is being infused with religious language, which is
reinforced by the garbled Biblical quotation, 'snare and
ashes in the mouth'. We have a sense of some part-under-
stood ritual which is going forward in relation to Patusan;
and indeed we shall see that there is considerable ritual
element in Jim's rulership and death at Patusan, just as
there was in his proscription. Then again, the 'irresponsive parties' are exactly what Jim finds in Patusan, and
their responsiveness does not grow greater with the
passage of time; for all the good that he does, for all his
efforts, at the latter end when he goes to Doramin there is
a total lack of response. Again, the laughable hyena suits

Rajah Allang better than the standard 'laughing hyena' for despite his predatory and in some senses terrifying nature he is and remains a figure of fun, whose presence, a gibbering caricature, serves but to render the tragedy of Patusan grotesque.

In this passage, then, as so often in *Lord Jim*, the reader sees more deeply than Marlow, who is content to dismiss as superficial what has, in its curious way, significance; as we have stressed repeatedly, there is in this novel extraordinarily little that is irrelevant to the principal theme.

From this let us pass to the function of language in the speeches of Stein. With Stein we enter upon a different function of this technique of broken language, and one whose effect is dubious. Stein's interview with Marlow lies at the centre of the book, both formally and thematically, for it is he who is, more than any other character, the interpreter of Jim, of the actions and words which go forward, to us as readers. It is important to us that his utterances should be coherent and comprehensible; the fact that they are manifestly not so is one of the weaknesses of Conrad's handling of speech in this novel. More than structural defects in *Lord Jim*, I think that the feeling of dissatisfaction which has been so often traced in this work has its origins in Conrad's inability to express clearly what the central characters are saying. This may be, as we shall suggest, because he wants thereby to convey the impossibility of saying adequately all that there is to be said about Jim, whether as an individual or as a human being; or it may be that he has attempted to say something and failed. The fact remains that at crucial points in the narrative Conrad's language breaks down and becomes woolly. This is particularly noticeable in regard to Stein and to his

speeches. We see that at times Marlow can be woolly and
vague, and that his fumblings often occur at some crucial
point; and this vagueness is further complicated in the
case of Stein by the fact that he can as it were hide behind
the fact of his foreignness. After the first crisp diagnosis of
the problem (with which we shall deal in a moment) Stein
drifts off into generalizations and into incomprehensibili-
ties:

> I tell you my friend, it is not good for you to find you
> cannot make your dream come true, for the reason that
> you not strong enough are, or not clever enough. Ja!
> . . . and all the time you are such a fine fellow, too!
> Wie? Was? Gott in Himmel! How can that be? Ha! ha!
> ha!
> (xx.)

Now this is to no small extent redundant. The somewhat
theatrical German, and the Germanization of the English,
serves here no greatly useful purpose. When, then, we
come to really important parts of Stein's words, such as
'The way is to the destructive element submit yourself . . .
In the destructive element immerse'—words which Conrad evidently regards as significant, since he repeats them
and has Marlow meditate upon them several times and try
to tease out their meaning, we find ourselves distracted
from the meaning by the oddness of the word-order. This
does not add in any way to the meaning, but rather does
disservice, in that it detracts from the stature of Stein by
placing him stylistically on a level with his renegade
fellow-countryman, the captain of the *Patna*. Nevertheless, there is significance in the use of the language, even if
it be used at times unfortunately, and this we can see more
clearly if we consider briefly the language of the French
lieutenant.

The French lieutenant is another character whose pronouncements are necessary and central to a right comprehension of the work. Here again we find that something of what he is saying is a little dissipated by Conrad's giving him Frenchified language: but in his case not so much is lost since Conrad evidently has more sympathy with the French language than with the German, and is using it to express something which he feels cannot be expressed as well in English. There are shades of meaning in the French (Conrad's first foreign language) which he is anxious to get across, and which he obviously feels to be important, in that he gives us what purports to be the original of some phrases of the Frenchman. These are, in fact, quite possibly the terms in which Conrad first thought of them when considering what he should write. His reflections are cast in a form eminently suited to the French analytical mind; the lieutenant separates out what he considers to be the essential things to be observed and expresses them in precise, epigrammatic form. His reflection, 'L'homme est né poltron', (xiii.) comes straight from the Age of Enlightenment, the age when it was thought that man could be analysed and discussed in neat, formal terms, the age of clarity of thought and expression. Stein, on the other hand, expresses himself in many cases in the obscure, half-mystical way of the nineteenth-century German Romantic. The attitudes of these two men, expressing 'international opinion', are expressive of two complementary views of man.

Stein's diagnosis of Jim, in its clipped, certain fashion, seems to sweep away the veil of mist in which we have hitherto seen Jim, seems to attach to Jim a label rather in the same way that each of Stein's butterflies receives its label. His subsequent utterances, however, tend to cause the mist to close in again. We are here confronted with the question 'How far are we justified in attaching such labels to a human character'? Is not Conrad's work rather, in that fumbling of language which many critics have detected as a fault in it, in its polyglot wordiness, a declaration of the ultimate failure of language in the presentation of man? Is he not saying that there can be no last word on Jim because words are in and of themselves insufficient to convey what Jim was? Thus Marlow's hesitancies, Stein's broken musings, the half-caste captain's curious English, the Frenchman's words, the ravings of the mad engineer—these, perhaps, are the statement of the impossibility of describing Jim. Against them we have the certainties: the 'good old parson' in his

> . . . inviolable shelter of his book-lined, faded and comfortable study, where for forty years he had conscientiously gone over and over again the round of his little thoughts about faith and virtue, about the conduct of life and the only proper manner of dying; where he had written so many sermons, where he sits talking to his boy . . .          (xxxvi.)

or the Court with its 'pointed questions', its 'terribly distinct questions', 'a question to the point'. Linguistic certainty seems to partner moral certitude in this book; and likewise the morally uncertain is hesitant in language. For language is the expression of definition, whereas everything about Jim is nebulous. Thus his response to those questions of the Court is noteworthy: he could reproduce the engineer's moaning for the benefit of this Court that wanted facts—'as if facts could explain anything!' Likewise we may note that the facts are described in terms of all the senses; not, that is to say, defined in the limits of language, but in the raw material of experience before it is reduced to language for the purposes of comprehension.

> The facts those men were so eager to know had been visible, tangible, open to the senses, occupying their place in space and time, requiring for their existence a fourteen-hundred-ton steamer and twenty-seven minutes by the watch; they made a whole that had features, shades of expression, a complicated aspect that could be remembered by the eye, and something else besides, something invisible, a directing spirit of perdition that dwelt within, like a malevolent soul in a detestable body. He was anxious to make this clear . . .                    (iv.)

Confusion and hesitancy of speech seem to be in Conrad an indication of that fumbling approach to the ultimately indescribable, indeed ineffable, which lies at the heart of every human being and which cannot be investigated beyond a certain point. Is there, indeed, any better description of Jim that can be found than Stein's simple assertion that he is a romantic? Probably not, for all Conrad's verbosity.

Let us now turn to Jim himself. It is noteworthy that in the language which Conrad uses of Jim, and especially that which he puts into his mouth, the essentially adolescent character of Jim is expressed in the phrases which he uses, the excited, boyish phrases, the 'public-school' language. It is no small part of Jim's tragedy that he is unable to grow out of the schoolboy stage, unable to express himself in any adult fashion. This leads others to misunderstand him, for they do not perceive that Jim's assumptions are still those of a boy; and conversely, he misunderstands them since he does not perceive developed meaning. For example:

'Jove:' he gasped out. 'It is noble of you!'
Had he suddenly put his tongue out at me in derision, I could not have felt more humiliated. I thought to myself, 'Serve me right for a sneaking humbug . . .'
(xvii.)

Marlow's reaction to Jim's words is to treat them as mockery: he accepts them as though they had been spoken derisively by an adult, and in his reflection unconsciously drops into the idiom which would underlie Jim's words if they had been spoken by an adult—say, by a young officer: 'sneaking humbug'. But they are in fact perfectly seriously meant, only couched in schoolboy language, as when just later on Jim says to Marlow, 'You are a brick'. His reaction to Stein's offer is similar:

This was his introduction to an old chap called Doramin—one of the principal men out there—a big pot—who had been Mr. Stein's friend in that country where he had all these adventures. Mr. Stein called him 'war-comrade'. War-comrade was good. Wasn't it? And didn't Mr. Stein speak English wonderfully well? Said he had learned it in Celebes—of all places! That was awfully funny. Was it not? He did speak with an accent—a twang—did I notice? That chap Doramin had given him the ring. They had exchanged presents when they parted for the last time. Sort of promising eternal friendship. He called it fine—did I not? They had to make a dash for dear life out of the country when that Mohammed—Mohammed—What's-his-name had been killed. I knew the story, of course. Seemed a beastly shame, didn't it? (xxiii.)

Now this is language straight out of the *Boy's Own Paper*. Comparison with any such adventure paper for boys of the period, or with Kipling's schoolboy tales (e.g. *Stalky & Co.*) will show that this is the accepted schoolboy jargon of the period (to some extent, of any period). To pick out a few of the more obvious phrases, we may notice 'an old chap'; 'a big pot'; 'all these adventures'; 'awfully funny'; 'sort of promising'; 'he called it fine'; 'beastly shame'. The language is juvenile; it is expressive of an undeveloped mind. Even when he is in his more serious moments, Jim never rises to really mature thinking, and this is well conveyed in the language. It is the attitude which Marlow takes towards him sometimes:

> I was oppressed by a sad sense of resigned wisdom, mingled with the amused and profound pity of an old man helpless before a childish disaster ... You had to listen to him as you would to a small boy in trouble. He didn't know. It had happened somehow. It would never happen again. (ix.)

> Next moment he looked a dear good boy in trouble, as before. (xvi.)

It is the attitude which Jewel discovers towards him when they address each other; 'Hello, girl!'—'Hello, boy!' Each of these two is innocent in every sense of the word. 'Arcadian' is the word which Marlow uses to describe their existence. Certainly there is little in their language to suggest any attachment stronger than that of the Children of the New Forest. It is this attitude of mind, the undeveloped, adolescent mind, that goes a long way towards explaining some of the puzzle of Jim.

## Descriptive Style

We have dealt so far with Conrad's style in passages of direct speech; and for this novel, where speech is so important in the revelation of character and in the evaluation of statements made, this must be our first concern. Nevertheless, it is principally for his descriptive passages that Conrad is particularly known: the expression 'Conradese' refers to this technique. It is a style which is found especially in the early works, in particular *Almayer's Folly*, and it consists in the main of a very heavy and languorous style, relying extensively upon adjectival constructions and, in verbs, the participial constructions. We may consider briefly some examples from various parts of *Lord Jim*: first from the description of the squall on board the *Patna*:

> First you see a darkening of the horizon—no more; then a cloud rises opaque like a wall. A straight edge of vapour lined with sickly whitish gleams flies up from the south-west, swallowing the stars in whole constellations; its shadow flies over the waters, and confounds sea and sky into one abyss of obscurity. And all is still. No thunder, no wind, no sound; not a flicker of lightning. Then in the tenebrous immensity a livid arch appears; a swell or two like undulations of the very darkness run past, and, suddenly, wind and rain strike together with a peculiar impetuosity as if they had burst through something solid. (ix.)

Here we have not the overloaded weight of adjective and noun constructions which is to be found in, for example the description of the Arabian Sea by night (Chapter iii, at the beginning). Yet the heaviness of the air is conveyed in the heavy constructions, using Romance words (an evidence of French thought in the writing). Such are 'confounds' (for 'blends') 'obscurity' (for 'darkness'), 'peculiar impetuosity' (for 'suddenness'). In giving these alternatives we do not mean to suggest that they express exactly what the Romance words convey; we merely indicate that there were other ways open to Conrad, which he rejected. That Conrad consciously used them, and used them, moreover, in contrast to the more simple way, is shown by the last part of the quotation: 'and, suddenly, wind and rain strike together . . . as if they had burst through something solid'. Here there is but one word which is not Saxon in derivation, 'solid', and this is so common that we are not conscious of its foreignness (as we are of, say, 'tenebrous'). Conrad opposes the two kinds of vocabulary in order to suggest the contrast between the heaviness of the air before the breaking of the storm and the sudden swiftness of the squall. It is a technique of management of vocabulary and rhythm which may be observed in many writers; a pattern for it is given, for example, in Pope's *Essay on Criticism*, a convenient memorandum for any study of English rhythm, whether in verse or prose.

This opposition of the heavy in vocabulary and rhythm in this passage is not confined to the last sentence; rather is it pervasive, suggesting the constant tension between the heavy calm and the bursting squall: thus, for example, in the sentence 'A straight edge . . . obscurity', we have the tense sounds of 'straight edge' set against the open 'vapour'; the slow heaviness of 'sickly whitish gleams' set against the quickness of 'flies up'; the violence of the unexpected verb 'swallowing the stars' against the calm which we expect of 'whole constellations'; the skimming rhythm of 'its shadow flies over the waters', and the clashing of 'compounds sea and sky' subsiding into the gloom of 'one abyss of obscurity' with its long open vowels. The feeling of the atmosphere in the passage is conveyed in negatives: 'No thunder, no wind, no sound; not a flicker of lightning'. (This technique of describing by negatives is found in Milton and Keats pre-eminently: compare with this passage the description of the Vale of Saturn in Keats's *Hyperion*.) These are favourite techniques with Conrad. Compare this passage, where Jim and Marlow look down from the heights upon Patusan:

> . . . below us stretched the land, the great expanse of the forests, sombre under the sunshine, rolling like a sea, with glints of winding rivers, the grey spots of villages, and here and there a clearing, like an islet of light amongst the dark waves of continuous tree-tops. A brooding gloom lay over this vast and monotonous landscape; the light fell on to it as if into an abyss. The land devoured the sunshine; only far off, along the coast, the empty ocean, smooth and polished within the faint haze, seemed to rise up to the sky in a wall of steel.
>
> (xxvi.)

Here again we have the heavy style for conveying foreboding. The sentences are piled up with phrases heavy with nouns and adjectives; the verbs are reduced to a minimum of active parts; participles and gerunds are substituted wherever possible. We notice again the use of the heavy open vowels; and this time we see that the vocabulary is by no means so noticeably Romance as in the former passage. Only the most ordinary words are used, and these by their very ordinariness convey the flatness and greyness of the land which Marlow is trying to put over to us. We note again the violent verb 'devoured the sunshine', and Conrad's favourite 'abyss'. Here we see also the retarding use of the genitive: 'of the forests'; 'of winding rivers'; 'of villages'; 'of light'; 'of

continuous tree-tops'; 'of steel'. The genitive construction with 'of' has the effect of giving to the phrase or
sentence in which it occurs a balance which serves to
retard the rhythm by introducing two elements of equal
weight; the repeated use of this construction, as here,
makes for great slowness in the rhythm of the sentence. It
is a variation of the equally heavy adjective and noun
construction, which is well seen in this last passage which
we shall consider, where Marlow, alone now, observes the
effect of the moon between the horns of the hill in Patusan:

> It threw its level rays afar as if from a cavern, and in this
> mournful eclipse-like light the stumps of felled trees
> uprose very dark, the heavy shadows fell at my feet on
> all sides, my own moving shadow, and across my path
> the shadow of the solitary grave perpetually garlanded
> with flowers. In the darkened moonlight the interlaced
> blossoms took on shapes foreign to one's memory and
> colours indefinable to the eye, as though they had been
> special flowers gathered by no man, grown not in this
> world, and destined for the use of the dead alone. Their
> powerful scent hung in the warm air, making it thick
> and heavy like the fumes of incense. The lumps of white
> coral shone round the dark mound like a chaplet of
> bleached skulls . . .                                   (xxxiv.)

In this passage it is evidently the monotonous weight of
the equal adjective and noun constructions which give it
the sombre and breathless tone which it possesses. Let us
consider how numerous they are: level rays; mournful
eclipse-like light; felled trees; heavy shadows; all sides;
moving shadow; solitary grave perpetually garlanded;
darkened moonlight; interlaced blossoms; shapes foreign;

colours indefinable; special flowers; powerful scent; warm air; white coral; dark mound; bleached skulls.

That is to say, within this comparatively short passage there are seventeen examples of this construction, not counting the constructions with the demonstrative adjectives; and of these seventeen fifteen are of two members only (i.e. adjective and noun.) Besides this, we have five examples of the partitive construction with 'of', and ten participles (as against six active verbs.) It is the equality of stress, as we have said, that causes sentences using these constructions to become heavy, and this is the most characteristic Conradian descriptive style in this period of his writing: the heavy, drowsy atmosphere of the East. If we consider the list we have made, there is nothing particularly striking about the words themselves or their combinations (except perhaps the oxymoron 'darkened moonlight')—there is no magic in the words. It is the syntax that makes the style, and this equilibrium of rhythm is the essence of 'Conradese'.

## Questions and Projects

1. Which parts of *Lord Jim* did you find relatively difficult to read and understand because of the manner of expression?

2. On the evidence of *Lord Jim* what would you take to be the merits and limitations of Conrad's use of English as a medium for a novel?

3. Do you find that the passages of direct speech are more successful than the narrative or descriptive passages in *Lord Jim*?

4. Show how Conrad makes speech reflect character in (a) Marlow (b) Stein (c) Jim.

E

5. Make a parallel list of reference to show where you think Conrad is (a) most and (b) least successful in communicating his material—narrative, moral, psychological—to the reader.

6. Make a varied collection of notable instances of imagery and its significance in *Lord Jim*.

# 5. SOME IMPORTANT IDEAS

*Lord Jim* is not only a yarn about one man, an extraordinary and lonely figure. It is a novel which lays claim to universal meaning; which purports to be saying, as indeed every significant work of literature must, something about the human condition. In particular, the problem of identity figures large in the book. We are shown a man without a name, set in a context where there is no room for the kind of isolation which his imagination ideally presents to him. In the situations in which he is placed, there is always this tension between the claims of the community, whether expressed in a code, such as the law, or the 'solidarity of the craft', or on the other hand less certainly expressed, as in the obligations of one human being, as it were Jim, towards another, as Jewel. Constantly we have laid before us the question of authority. Is there an authority which can claim obedience from every man; is there an external and compelling power, apart from the individual 'guardian angel' or 'familiar devil'? In *Lord Jim* several important notions are introduced, and remain throughout as standards, as principles by which we judge of the characters and their actions. These principles may be seen as opposing forces, which, simplified, can be thought of as Isolation and Community, Individualism and Solidarity, Duty and Imagination of the individual. In this section we shall examine some of these ideas, and see how the characters are fitted into the context of the principles which they represent.

*Duty*

As a captain of the Merchant Marine, Conrad is inclined to place weight upon duty done, and that often in terms of work done, over every other good. Indeed it may be said that Conrad is, more than any other writer, except perhaps Kipling, with whom he has many attitudes in common, the novelist of work. He views character neither in terms of intention nor in terms of words, but of action performed. In a novel where so much is concerned with appearance and reality, it is the words and the thoughts which are the appearance, the actions which are the reality against which those appearances are judged, and on the evidence of which Jim is finally to be judged. Conrad presents us with much talking, much searching, many opinions—his Marlow spends much of the book trying to plumb Jim's character by means of questioning, obtaining opinions, and thinking, often in a woolly-minded way which one critic has seen as expressing an essential indecision on the part of Conrad himself as to the final judgement to be made about Jim. But Marlow's indecision need not be ours. Thus, for example:

> The thing was always with me; I was always eager to take opinion on it, as though it had not been practically settled: individual opinion—international opinion, by Jove! That Frenchman's, for instance. His own country's pronouncement was uttered . . .          (xiv.)

> I felt as though I were taking professional opinion on the case. His imperturbable and mature calmness was that of an expert in possession of the facts, and to whom one's perplexities are mere child's play.          (xiii.)

> He had diagnosed the case for me, and at first I was quite startled to find how simple it was; and indeed our

conference resembled so much a medical consultation
... that it seemed natural to ask, 'What's good for
it?'                                                    (xx.)

Nevertheless, it is on the basis of the facts, as may be seen
from the second quotation, that judgement is to be made,
and if Marlow endeavours by 'taking opinion' to evade
the pronunciation of the final judgement, we are set as the
'experts in posession of the facts'.

The technique will be familiar to readers of Chaucer's
General Prologue to *The Canterbury Tales*. The Chaucerian
narrator is an untrustworthy judge, and his opinion is not
to be accepted—our judgement is based upon deciding
whether the facts presented to us, the actions which the
characters are shown to be performing or to have performed, are or are not consonant with the appearance
which they present. Thus we distinguish between the
Knight and the Parson on the one hand and the Monk and
the Friar on the other. So here: circumlocution as prac-
tised by Jim cannot blind us to the facts. The what, and
not the why, is the final test of judgement.

When we come then to examine these facts, we perceive that Stein's diagnosis of romanticism fits not the
why alone, but the what. This is true as well of the evidently good actions as of the palpably bad. If dereliction
of duty be a prime factor in the condemnation of Jim's
jumping from the *Patna*, we may say that it is so also in his
final sacrifice of himself. We may say this because the code
of duty is based upon service, not to any ideal of heroism,
but to utility. Heroism is admirable, but utility is prized
and commended. Ideals are for Conrad shifty, nebulous
things, which have only value in so far as they can be
measured in terms of work, action and utility. In this

respect Jim's final action, like his first, is a dereliction of duty brought about by his failure to recognize wherein and to what his duty lies. If there be authority, it is that of solidarity to 'the craft' with all the implications of work which that conveys. To Jim, however, there is no higher authority than himself to which duty is owed.

Let us consider his period in Patusan. There he has and owes duties which are not so obvious as those aboard ship. In the last resort, as on board ship, Jim's duty is shown to be to himself. Marlow, it will be remembered, cannot make him see the enormity of his jumping except in terms of a 'chance missed'—there is no sense of responsibility to others, whether that of common humanity, towards the pilgrims; of discipline, towards his captain; or of his calling, towards the vessel. (Marlow, on the other hand, is very responsible towards his calling—consider, for example, his remarks concerning those whom he has trained. But Marlow also feels a higher responsibility, towards the country, seen as a maritime power—see his 'spirit of the land' speech.) As regards a higher authority than those commonly accepted by seamen, an authority embodied for Marlow in the spirit of the land, it is not entirely clear what Jim feels. He seems to acknowledge that there is a sort of judgement to be passed and an external authority which may pass it; he recognizes that he cannot go back, that there are people 'out there' before whom he is 'not good enough'. There is also the influence of his father to be considered. This is somewhat difficult to assess. The preservation of the last letter seems to acknowledge the authority of the 'easy morality . . . &c.' which is the foundation of the force which binds 'us'—on the other hand, Jim's remarks that 'they would not understand' in a way suggests that he is rejecting 'their' conceptions in favour of his own which he still considers to be higher in essence than those accepted by mankind as represented by his father and Marlow, with the authorities, civil and moral, for which they stand. In this spirit he takes it upon himself to die.

There is, I maintain, no duty upon him to die other than that imposed by his own exalted conceptions of himself as the stainless hero. It is a death to redeem himself to himself, not to redeem himself before the outside world which has rejected him for his first failure, as he thinks.

For what does he die? Again, our answer must depend on the facts presented, and here we can say that it is the blindness induced by his romanticism which leads him to mistake his true duty and to substitute for it his own egoism. But he had several duties: to Stein, to Jewel, to the colony, to Marlow and the 'spirit of the land', even, as well as to Doramin. All these duties were on different planes of cogency, and each had its claim on Jim. The fact that he saw only the duty to Doramin to the exclusion of all others, saw, that is, the only one which would involve his egotistically romantic nature in what it would consider a worthy action, is a measure of his blindness to true duty and thus of his ultimate irresponsibility.

This attitude of being responsible to himself only is a feature of his whole life—it appears, for example, in his scorning of the boy on the training vessel who had saved the drowning man; in his rejection of the Court's authority; in his treatment of Marlow's paper-mill-owning friend; and in his treatment of Egstrøm and Blake, as well as in Patusan. In his construction of his own world in Patusan, he considered none of the external claims which were to be made upon him. He controls Rajah Allang, has a fort in the Colonial manner, and plays rather the colonial viceroy indeed than the commercial trader. This measures up to his own feelings about himself, and he comes to Doramin at the latter end in the role of the lord, Tuan Jim, coming to pay a personal debt to his people.

But his judgement about the death of Dain Waris and his responsibility for it is in its way as wrong as his views about the jumping. In his reaction he mistakes the import and obligations of the feudal position, in which he finds himself, and substitutes for it a notion of honour which is typical of a period of aristocratic decadence. The warriors who gathered round the body of Byrhtnoth at the battle of Maldon would not have understood Jim's attitude; the courtiers of Lewis XV of France, or the officers of William II of Prussia might well have done. For the death of Dain Waris was the result of an error of judgement on Jim's part, not of a moral fault, as Jim sees it, and in these terms he pays for it. Anyone might have been deceived by Brown's story, knowing nothing of the facts of his life—again we have presented to us the pre-importance of facts over words. Anyone, that is, even one whose conscience was not fortuitously pricked by Brown's words, might have made the same mistake, for mistake it was, depending on the incalculable factor of the inter-meddling of Cornelius.

Here we have a beautifully presented contrast between the first and second failure of Jim in terms of fact, significance and interpretation. Whereas to jump from the *Patna*, abandoning the ship and one's duty, was a moral fault which Jim persists in seeing in terms of an error of judgement, a 'chance missed', the affair with Brown resulting in the death of Dain Waris is an error of judgement which Jim regards as a moral fault. Abandoning the *Patna* was, as is quite evident, a dereliction of duty and hence a moral fault, on several counts. But to permit Brown to go peacefully was not dereliction of duty, but rather discharging it—discharging the duty of assistance to one's fellow-countryman in distress, discharging the duty of maintaining the peace in the colony. Afterwards, when this had resulted in an ill outcome, to accept the sort of responsibility for the death of Dain Waris which Jim feels it incumbent upon him to accept, serves but to discharge a personal debt of honour between Doramin and himself. It disregards the duty which he owes to the colony at large, in that when his protection is removed, the rapacious forces of Rajah Allang will be enabled once more to oppress the people; it disregards the duty which he owes to Stein to develop Patusan commercially, a duty which requires the setting aside of personal considerations; and it disregards the duty which he owes to Jewel which is, equally with that owed to Doramin, a personal duty, but one which is bound up with human feeling and not with abstract notions of honour. Just as Jewel's father had done, Jim places this abstract notion over the human duty to the loved one. The problem is no new one; it is found in Corneille's heroes seeking *gloire*; in Wolfram von Eschenbach's Gaheret and Herzeloide; in Virgil's Aeneas and Dido; in Homer's Odysseus and Nausicaa. In these cases, the personal failure is condoned or condemned as it serves to further a wider good or not; in Conrad, where the hero is no personal hero, but is subject to the wider and communal obligations of a body, whether 'the craft', 'us', 'the land' or mankind at large, this sort of personal failure of duty cannot but be condemned.

Were Jim's failures, as Marlow and Stein propound, the result of too much imagination? The contrast with the native helmsman would seem to suggest it. The jumping resulted from a weakness which opposed what Jim saw himself as being; the offering of himself to be shot was the result of acting on his own ideas falsely. In each case there is a fiction presented by Jim's imagination which he sees as the truth, and which not only causes him to act in a false way, but prevents his acting in a true way. The helmsman, on the other hand, totally devoid of imagination, stuck to his post and did the right thing. Asked by the Court what he thought 'he says he thought nothing'. Is this blankness a fault? In Conrad's view, based as I think it is on the utility of actions, it gains a higher place over Jim's imaginative failures. Compare the figure of the captain in Conrad's *Typhoon*, sailing his vessel blandly through the centre of the storm, devoid of the imaginative power to perceive what must be the consequences, what it will be like. This unimaginative quality saves him. Here again Conrad's attitude seems to be that the thing done is more important than the reason for it; and in *Lord Jim* this involves us in an evaluative division between duty and imagination, where the force of duty compels to right action, and the vivid realization of danger evoked by imagination restrains from the right and impels to the wrong. Imagination always sees itself as doing the right thing, and shrinks at the pinch, finding excuses for inaction; duty does what it has to do and thinks nothing. Conrad's view of duty appears to involve an implicit condemnation of imagination.

We may see the result of the action of imagination to undermine duty in the figure of Brierly. That there is a moral failure in Brierly's case seems certain:

> No wonder Jim's case bored him, and while I thought with something akin to fear of the immensity of his

contempt for the young man under examination, he
was probably holding silent enquiry into his own case.
The verdict must have been of unmitigated guilt . . .
(vi.)

Brierly is altogether something of an enigma, at first
glance. There is a distinctly perceptible sneer in Marlow's
words as he speaks of Brierly's accomplishments and
honours, of his command, of his awards for seamanship
and courage—how is this to be taken in view of our statement of Conrad's ideas concerning utility and devotion to
duty as the highest good? We must, however, consider
that the judgement of him, like Marlow's recollection of
his last conversation with Brierly 'is tinged with the
knowledge of the end that followed so close upon it'. (vi.)
This end, the suicide, is a dereliction of duty in spite of
the fact that everything is left arranged for the orderly
sailing of the vessel and the disposal of affairs afterwards.
It is a desertion and abandonment, not so much, as in Jim's
case, of an actual vessel in a physical emergency as of that
ill-defined but omnipresent idea which lies behind all
Conrad's words about the 'craft of the sea' which makes a
man 'fit to live or die as the sea may decree' (v.)—but not
as he himself may.

*Imagination*
    Here we must ask what sort of imagination it is that is
condemned, for it seems unlikely that the total unthink-
ingness of the native helmsman is the state of which
Conrad finally approves. Rather is he an extreme, used for
the purpose of setting off Jim's over-indulgence in thought
at the expense of action. In a somewhat similar use of this
technique may be seen the figure of Chester. Here we have
another comparison to aid us—Brierly, whose negligent

attitude at the trial of Jim concealed, so Marlow declares, a silent trial of himself. Here we see the fatal effects of too much imagination, too much thought, upon a man not, like Jim, a failure and a traitor, but rather, in the eyes of the world a success, and in his own eyes the most important and admirable man alive.

> At thirty-two he had one of the best commands going in the Eastern trade—and, what's more, he thought a lot of what he had. There was nothing like it in the world, and I suppose if you had asked him point-blank he would have confessed that in his opinion there was not such another commander. The choice had fallen upon the right man. The rest of mankind that did not command the sixteen-knot steel steamer *Ossa* were rather poor creatures.                    (vi.)

He wishes to patronize Marlow, who shrugs him off:

> ... when I reflected that I was associated in these fatal disadvantages with twelve hundred millions of other more or less human beings, I found that I could bear my share of his good-natured and contemptuous pity ...                    (vi.)

In this good-humoured irony of Marlow we have the clue to Brierly's character, and through that to Jim's. Brierly, like Jim, is an immense egoist. He thinks in terms of 'Montague Brierly, in command of the *Ossa* ... &c.' rather than in terms of that human commonalty which is expressed by Marlow in his 'twelve hundred millions of other more or less human beings', which is symbolized in little by the community of the sea and the spirit of the land, and which is sustained by the 'easy morality and family news' of the parsonage. (xxxvi.)

These men, Brierly and Jim, are figures; 'untroubled shapes, with a stern and romantic aspect' if you will, but men cut off from the community of existence by their own massive egoism, and more than half willing their own isolation. They represent the Byronic hero set satirically in the real world.

The development of the figure of the Byronic hero in nineteenth-century fiction has been traced by Mario Praz in *The Romantic Agony*. It was a figure which aroused unbounded admiration or detestation according to the temperament of the writer treating of it. For Conrad, the isolated, superhuman image of the Romantic, more specifically the Byronic hero, was not admirable. He was to be shunned as having placed himself outside the community of mankind, not glorified for it. This exclusion from the human community is represented in Jim's case symbolically by his lack of a surname, of that which expresses formally the family and wider social relationships. He possesses but the forename, the personal. His fate, too, is discovered in the words of Jones to Marlow concerning Brierly:

'Ay, ay! neither you nor I, sir, had ever thought so much of ourselves.'                                                    (vi.)

This is seen to be the paralysing and destructive force which operates upon Brierly and Jim. In their deaths, each has a reason which, in Marlow's words 'wasn't anything which would have disturbed much either of us two'. (vi.) It is this egoism which consists in thinking so much of ourselves, which is the enfeebling and finally destructive force. There is a great irony in Conrad's placing of these two splendid egoists in such a relationship as that of the trial, where the moral failure of both worldly success and worldly failure is seen to be the same. There is a similarly ironic positioning of characters at the end when, in Patusan, Brown and Jim are placed in somewhat the same position.

For both Brierly and Jim, the force of imagination causes them to ignore the facts of their situation. They set aside the facts and judgements of the community in which they find themselves for the sake of a vain confidence of private revelation. Thus we are left to guess at a reason for Brierly's suicide; Jones's words, however, strongly suggest the force of imagination.

Conrad's view of Imagination is further seen in his remarks on Jim's apprentice experience, when he lies in his bunk, disabled by a spar, during the storm:

> The danger, when not seen, has the imperfect vagueness of human thought. The fear grows shadowy: and Imagination, the father of all terrors, unstimulated, sinks to rest in the dulness of exhausted emotion.    (ii.)

Marlow calls Jim an 'imaginative beggar', and goes on to define the meaning of this imagination expressed in effect.

> Ah, he was an imaginative beggar! He would give himself away; he would give himself up. I could see in his glance darted into the night all his inner being carried on, projected headlong into the fanciful realm of heroic speculation.    (vii.)

It is this sort of language which is ever used about Jim, and its connotations are supported by the facts as we are shewn them. Take, for example, the presentation of him as a boy on the training-ship failing to jump into the cutter at the right time, being held in awe by the raging of the elements:

There was a fierce purpose in the gale, a furious earnestness in the screech of the wind, in the brutal tumult of earth and sky, that seemed directed at him, and made him hold his breath in awe. He stood still. It seemed to him that he was being whirled around.   (i.)

We may note here the frequent use of verbs such as *seem*, *appear* in this passage and in others concerning Jim, and a further syntactical device for creating the world of illusion in which Jim lives—the device of reported speech or reported thought, which means that the author is not compelled to vouch for the objective truth of the statements so made. In the passage we have just quoted, the first sentence is not objective, but the report of Jim's subjective impressions. In a more highly-inflected language than ours the sentence would be in the subjunctive. By the use of such devices Conrad conveys to us the unreality of the world of Jim's imagination.

The readily impressible Jim thus succumbs to inaction as his imagination gets to work—in a passage of almost poetic force of description—on the storm and the glimpsed sights of the works of man apparently cast topsy-turvy by the force of Nature. Always this is something which impresses him, and each time that he allows himself to be so impressed he is deceived. He sees:

The small craft jumbled and tossing along the shore . . . the broad ferry-boats pitching ponderously at anchor, the vast landing-stages heaving up and down and smothered in sprays. The next gust seemed to blow all this away.
(i.)

Yet the anchors hold, the old training-ship, though quivering, bows but gently head to wind, and the song of her youth at sea in the rigging recalls the times that she has been through this before. Afterwards, Jim is forced to see that his awe has been of an 'inefficient menace'. Likewise, when he is on the *Patna*, it is his lack of trust in the old iron bulkhead, whose instability appears to him to be confirmed by the falling flake of rust, that puts him again in the position of one paralysed, awed by the potentiality of Nature, which is shown to be (like his own heroism) a spurious menace, an unrealized possibility of danger, an appearance which never becomes reality. On the training-ship, on the vessel which takes him out to the East, on the *Patna*, the works of man in their workmanship are tested and found strong, but Jim has doubted them, and remained inactive. To his imagination it is the great forces of Nature which are resistless. Men with less imagination trust to the frail but capable works of men, as they trust to their fellow-men in the company of the sea, and come through without, apparently, thinking much about it. The bowman in the cutter, the 'boy with a face like a girl's and big grey eyes' (i.) (cp. 'Jim kept his freshness in the climate. Had he been a girl . . . one would have said that he was blooming . . . (xviii.)) thinks of his experience in terms of immediate and active impressions —Old Symons swearing, grasping his leg, the boathook, the rescued man's cries and fainting, the blood—and these trivia (in comparison with the gale) preserve him from the inactivity which is the result of the imaginative contemplation of universals.

'What business had he to be imaginative?' cries Marlow. This contrast between business and imagination represents in a way Conrad's judgement on Jim's imagination, for in the world which Jim has accepted in going to sea, the business is more important than the imagination. In a way, Chester is right in saying that the important thing is to be able to see things as they are (the irony is that he himself is blind to the impracticality of his schemes). This attitude is present also in other novels of Conrad, as for example in *Typhoon*, where the obstinate, thoughtless, unimaginative captain comes through by the exercise of his 'business' qualities, his seamanship, and by not giving way to the terrors of the imagination. The important thing is getting on with the job.

*Isolation and Community—the 'One Of Us' Image*

Jim's romanticism is described in Romantic terms, and these are constantly opposed to the real thoughts and words of men. From the beginning we have this contrast, with its implicit condemnation of the romantic:

> They said, 'Confounded fool!' as soon as his back was turned. This was their criticism on his exquisite sensibility. (i.)

> 'He was the mate of the *Patna* that voyage,' I said, feeling that I owed some explanation. For a time Egstrøm remained very still, with his fingers plunged in his hair at the side of his face, and then exploded. 'And who the devil cares about that?'—'I daresay, no one', I began . . . 'And what the devil is he—anyhow —for to go on like this?' (xviii.)

> This last affair (*sc. at Schomberg's where he fought the Dane*) however, made me seriously uneasy, because if his exquisite sensibilities were to go the length of involving him in pot-house shindies, he would lose his name of an inoffensive, if aggravating fool, and acquire that of a common loafer. (xix.)

F

The exquisite sensibility of the Romantic, of the Byronic hero is measured against the world of fact and ridiculed by comparison. In a world of 'Confounded fools!', 'What the devils!' and 'pot-house shindies' the sensibility of Jim wilts and fades away. It is ridiculed and condemned, not so much for what it is ('inoffensive, if aggravating') but for what it does. As a result of it, other men are put to practical inconvenience (Schomberg has to send to Europe for a new billiard cue to replace the one Jim broke in his fight) and these inconveniences, petty as they are, are used as a measure, and a degrading measure, of Jim's ideas and sensibilities. The fact that such things as broken billiard cues can be seen to exist in Jim's world is enough to bring down the whole romantic edifice. Schomberg may be a petty man with small ideas, but the fact remains that his concern is to get a new billiard cue. Such is the effect of Jim's indulgence of his personal romanticism at the expense of communal obligations. Likewise, not considering his obligations, Jim walks out of the water-clerk's job at Egstrøm and Blake's, leaving Egstrøm in an awkward situation. But the last blow to the Byronic image is that as this lonely figure wanders brooding over his secret round the Eastern seas, all the while his lonely secret is really public property:

> For instance, in Bangkok, where he found employment with Yucker Brothers, charterers and teak merchants, it was almost pathetic to see him go about in sunshine hugging his secret, which was known to the very up-country logs on the river. Schomberg, the keeper of the hotel where he boarded, a hirsute Alsatian of manly bearing and an irrepressible retailer of all the scandalous gossip of the place, would, with both elbows on the

table, impart an adorned version of the story to any
guest who cared to imbibe knowledge along with the
more costly liquors. 'And, mind you, the nicest fellow
you could meet,' would be his generous conclusion,
'quite superior.' (xix.)

The last word in this quotation, 'superior' is a beautiful
instance of the power of satirical belittling of false pom-
posity which Conrad possesses. To trace the history of the
use of the word in a poetic context (from such things as
Thomson's 'Man superior walks Amid the glad creation')
and in a social context ('a superior kind of upper servant')
to its use here would take too long; but the blend of
patronising ascendency given to Schomberg with the
echoes of the older poetic use forms a devastating criticism
on the Jim who has fallen from his exalted heights.

If the effect of imagination upon Jim is to paralyse him
and the possibility of action which he might have under-
taken, the reaction is to produce in him a feeling of self-
sufficiency and also, curiously, a feeling that he is all the
more attached to the code which is Marlow's. He views
his failures not as such, but as an increase in his own
potentialities for what shall be the supreme test (which he
mistakenly thinks himself to have found in his last
defiant gesture in Patusan). He fails in the cutter, but has
'enlarged his knowledge':

Otherwise he was rather glad he had not gone into the
cutter, since a lower achievement had served the turn.
He had enlarged his knowledge more than those who
had done the work. When all men flinched, then—he
felt sure—he alone would know how to deal with the
spurious menace of wind and seas. He knew what to
think of it. (i.)

Similarly he views the disastrous jump from the *Patna* as remediable; remediable, that is, in terms of that code of the seafaring community which would have had him remain in the first place. Whereas there is a feeling among Schomberg and Egstrøm and their fellows that the jump does not matter, and even Marlow from time to time feels that Jim attaches too much weight to it, nevertheless there is a very definite sense in which the jump is not remediable, and in which he is cast out from the community. 'There was always a doubt of his courage. The truth seems to be that it is impossible to lay the ghost of a fact.' (xix.) Marlow would not trust a ship to him, and both discover acute embarrassment when Jim takes passage in Marlow's vessel after having left the paper-mill. In terms of the craft which he has betrayed, his sin cannot be atoned for. So the weight of moral judgement is removed from the terms of seamen's judgement and placed in the context of a more general judgement, in a wider community. Less is heard, in the part of the book after that passage in Marlow's vessel, of the solidarity of the craft, and with the Patusan section the images of authority change and become those of, for example, 'the spirit of the land', 'they': when Jim, as he parts from Marlow for the last time, begins to say, 'Tell them . . .' he is implicitly acknowledging the judgement of the outside world, which is different from, though related to 'the craft of the sea'—which is as it were a microcosm. (Marlow allegorizes the boat as the microcosm in Chapter x.) The whole question of loyalty shifts from that of the seaman towards his craft to the wider community. Jim is said to be 'one of us'.

He was, of course, 'one of us', in terms of the craft of the sea, too, but in a sense somewhat narrowed down by the loyalty within the wider loyalty which is now to be examined. This is symptomatic of the general widening of the horizons which characterizes the second part of the book, that set in Patusan.

What, then, or who are these 'us' of whom Marlow so often speaks? Plainly they do not constitute seamen only, nor is every seaman 'one of us'—there are for example, those who have opted out, such as the men at the hospital, or the Danish officer of the King of Siam, or Chester and Brown. 'One of us' has evidently connotations both moral and social.

There is the acceptance of the code of honour of a gentleman—which is to say, of something which is never defined or discussed but taken, as the French officer takes it, so much for granted, so much as a thing which one possesses naturally, that he can say nothing concerning its loss. The book is written and addressed with certain assumptions of shared ideas between the reader and the characters. This is one of the functions of the audience of Marlow—perhaps most eminently so in the case of the 'privileged man' who reads Marlow's final despatch. If on the one hand they are meant to offer some sort of partial interpretation, a little in the manner of the Greek chorus (although their presence in *Lord Jim* is not as much felt in this respect as it is, say, in *Heart of Darkness*) another function is certainly that of being our representatives in the story. They carry with them 'our' attitudes, they stand for us as readers—and by this function they also compel us, whatever our private views, to accept, at least temporarily, and within the context of the novel, the code which is based on this concept of 'us'.

But the whole concept of 'one of us', whatever it may immediately mean to Marlow, Charley and the others there, is shown to be wider than this. The concept grows during the novel, and grows into a symbol, so that the community thereby expressed is no longer that of the comradeship of the sea merely, or that of belonging to a particular social pattern at all, but rather that of common humanity. Jim's dreams and their reality, his failures and his desire for measurement and judgement are seen as those of humanity at large rather than of a somewhat peculiar individual. Jim's 'fearless glance to left and right' (xlv.) is a demand to be judged, not only by those to whom he is 'not good enough', the English or the Europeans, but by his fellow men, in whose eyes he desires to prove himself. His desire is never, for example, seen in terms of the sea: when he has experienced his first failure, on board the training vessel, the situation of which he dreams is

> When all men flinched, then—he felt sure—he alone would know how to deal with the spurious menace of wind and seas. (i.)

(Is there here, perhaps, a reminiscence of Kipling's *If*?) He dismisses the Court's jurisdiction and evidently sees himself and his role in wider terms.

But if he is a representative of common humanity, then it is as the representative of erring humanity that he is here shown. Moreover, it is precisely his lack of community, his egoism, which is his frailty, which separates him, and which makes him in a deeper sense than the fact of the jump 'not good enough'. In effect his refusal to go back, his refusal to face 'them', to say anything to 'them', has something of the same tone as Coriolanus' 'I banish you'. To Jim, it is ever the world that has failed him, rather than he who has failed the world.

He felt angry with the brutal tumult of earth and sky
for taking him unawares and checking unfairly a
generous readiness for narrow escapes.                    (i.)

'I had to look at all that,' he said . . . 'Was there ever
any one so shamefully tried!'                             (ix.)

'It is so difficult—so awfully unfair—so hard to understand . . . I was so lost, you know. It was the sort of thing
one does not expect to happen to one. It was not like a
fight, for instance.'                                     (xi.)

It is therefore another excellent irony that places Jim in
his final relationship with Brown, that supreme egoist, an
egoist greater even than Jim, who finally brings about
Jim's destruction. Brown is a decayed specimen of 'one of
us'. His 'title', Gentleman, expresses, as Stewart says, the
state from which he has fallen, a state which was used
as the unspoken standard. But Brown, exaggerated pic-
ture as he is, does but put into brutal practice attitudes
which are essentially similar to those of Jim.

What distinguished him from his contemporary brother
ruffians . . . was the arrogant temper of his misdeeds
and a vehement scorn for mankind at large and for his
victims in particular. The others were merely vulgar
and greedy brutes, but he seemed moved by some
complex intention. He would rob a man as if only to
demonstrate his poor opinion of the creature. . . .
                                                       (xxxviii')

There was in the broken, violent speech of that man,
unveiling before me his thoughts with the very hand of
Death upon his throat, an undisguised ruthlessness of
purpose, a strange vengeful attitude towards his own

past, and a blind belief in the righteousness of his will
against all mankind . . .                                    (xl.)

Neither Brown nor Jim has any real regard for the world
as such, although each accepts the regard of the world as
necessary and desirable. Upon each is a title put—Gentleman Brown, Lord Jim. As Brown's title of gentleman
is ironically given, so the title of lord is seen to be a mis-
nomer for Jim. The function of the lord is social, is one of
protection, which Jim fails to give to his people—and
fails twice, the first time because of his error of judgement
in the matter of Brown, the second when he voluntarily
removes the protection in the name of his own conception
of honour. It is in a sense the old problem which is first
handled in English by the author of *Beowulf*—the respec-
tive obligations of the hero and the king. For Jim's death
is conceived in terms of heroism—and such is also his
view of his other trials. Heroism, however, is something
essentially personal and independent—the hero is bound
by no tie of responsibility to a community in his actions. If
he succeed, he succeeds for himself, and if he fail, his
failure touches himself alone. But Jim is never placed in
such a situation where these preconditions for the heroic
would apply. He is placed always in the communal context: whether that of the shipboard or that of the colony.
He always has responsibility, which he always evades; he
seeks to place himself in the hero's position, and this
chance is never given him. In the end, therefore, he seeks
out and meets, as it were, his unnecessary dragon.

One of the contrasts of appearance and reality which is
especially notable structurally is the constant play and
tension between Jim's heroic idea of himself, which is
presented almost in the terms of romance, (where the

incident on the training ship would represent the *enfance*, the voyage out the initiation, the *Patna* the manhood, the drifting round the East the voyage, Patusan the rulership and death) and the unheroic context around him. Here personal heroism is scarcely possible, unless to the unimportant—to Bob Stanton, say, or to the French lieutenant —and the all-important thing is 'solidarity' to one's particular 'craft' or society—solidarity, perhaps, with the spirit of the land. Jim's failure to achieve his own ideals is in part at least occasioned by the impossibility in this world which Conrad presents to us of their accomplishment. Jim waits for the chance which can never come, and his only valuable work is done when, abandoning for the moment his ideas of personal glory, he arranges things in Patusan. Even here, however, there is an unresolved dichotomy. It is symbolized for Marlow in the mountain between whose horns the moon is to be seen:

> The appearance from the settlement is of one irregularly conical hill split in two, with the two halves leaning slightly apart. (xxi.)

Marlow and Jim stand together and watch the moon rise between the horns of the hill; as it escapes 'from a yawning grave in gentle triumph' Marlow has the feeling:

> . . . as though he had had a hand in regulating that unique spectacle. He had regulated so many things in Patusan! things that would have appeared as much beyond his control as the motions of moon and stars. (xxi.)

But when Marlow sees the moon alone, it wears a threatening aspect:

For a moment it looked as though the smooth disk, falling from its place in the sky upon the earth, had rolled to the bottom of that precipice: its ascending movement was like a leisurely rebound; it disengaged itself from the tangle of twigs; the base contorted line of some tree, growing on the slope, made a black crack right across its face. (xxxiv.)

Is it not possible to see this as an image of the flawed nature of Jim; of the contradictions which we have mentioned, of the split in him between desire and action, possibility and reality, between, perhaps, the inevitable demands of the world and the ideal singularity of himself?

We have spoken of Jim constantly as the great egoist, and seen in his egoism his downfall. It is, indeed, the primary characteristic of him, in his good as well as in his bad actions. Recklessness of personal safety in his occupation as a water-clerk is coupled with an equal recklessness of the safety of those under his command:

'That's a reckless sort of a lunatic you've got for a water-clerk, Egstrøm . . . two frightened niggers in the bottom boards, a yelling fiend at the tiller . . . Kick the niggers—out reefs—a squall on at the time— . . .' (xviii.)

And his time of greatness in Patusan is seen by Marlow, the companiable, solid Marlow, as a time also of loneliness:

He appeared like a creature not only of another kind but of another essence. (xxii.)

. . . he seemed to love the land and the people with a sort of fierce egoism, with a contemptuous tenderness. (xxiv.)

I can't with mere words convey to you the impression of his total and utter isolation. I know, of course, he was in every sense alone of his kind there, but the unsuspected qualities of his nature had brought him in such close touch with his surroundings that this isolation seemed only the effect of his power. His loneliness added to his stature. There was nothing within sight to compare him with ...                                    (xxvii.)

In this isolation lies the possibility both of his greatness and of his failure. It is his inability to associate himself with others which continually brings him down. In the training ship 'there was a fierce purpose in the gale ... that seemed directed at him ... he stood still ... Nevertheless he brooded apart that evening ... and the final effect of a staggering event was that, unnoticed and apart from the noisy crowd of boys, he exulted with fresh certitude in his avidity for adventure, and in a sense of many-sided courage.' (i.) In the ship out to the East: 'He lay there battened down in the midst of a small devastation, and felt secretly glad that he had not to go on deck'. (ii.) In the *Patna*: 'It is more than probable he thought himself cut off from them by a space that could not be traversed, by an obstacle that could not be overcome, by a chasm without bottom. He was as far as he could get from them—the whole breadth of the ship'. (xi.) And earlier, '... those men did not belong to the world of heroic adventure ... the quality of these men did not matter; he rubbed shoulders with them, but they could not touch him; he shared the air they breathed, but he was different ...' (iii.) Marlow too is struck by this difference, which he expresses as isolation, or as something indefinable about Jim. But the most important statement of Marlow's sense of the difference, perhaps, comes when he first sees Jim: it is a statement which links at once this difference and the sense of community expressed in 'one of us' in such a way as to reinterpret the difference, or rather to express what it ought to have been.

> He looked as unconcerned and unapproachable as only the young can look . . . He had no business to look so sound. I thought to myself,—Well, if this sort can go wrong like that . . . and I felt as though I could fling down my hat and dance on it from sheer mortification . . . I liked his appearance; he came from the right place; he was one of us. (v.)

To Marlow this that he ought to have been is perhaps more important than what he was:

> He stood there for all the parentage of his kind, for men and women by no means clever or amusing, but whose very existence is based upon honest faith, and upon the instinct of courage . . . he was outwardly so typical of that good, stupid kind we like to feel marching right and left of us in life . . . (v.)

In this latter quotation the reference of the idea 'one of us' is made very wide indeed. It expresses Marlow's belief in Jim's essential kinship with his fellow-men—a belief which, perhaps, Jim himself does not share. Indeed, throughout we are faced with the question whether Marlow's identification of Jim with the rest of humanity is in fact correct, or whether Jim is truly the Byronic, lonely figure as which he would like to see himself. Are we presented with an individual mystery, or with a figure for our own experience? We have cited several parallel treatments in other authors which seem to suggest that the problem at least is not new, and there may be some common ground for estimating Jim. Let us, then, pursue this useful term which Marlow introduces, and which in his later introduction to the novel Conrad stresses, 'one of us'.

Marlow first introduces the term, 'one of us', which has such importance in the evaluation of Jim, when he is describing his (but not our) first sight of Jim on the quayside (*vid. sup.*)—here we have the instant recognition of community, the acknowledgement of a bond and responsibility towards Jim in the name of that which governs them both. The idea of being 'my brother's keeper' is raised, although Marlow later disclaims it:

> I do not mean to imply that I figured to myself the spirit of the land uprising above the white cliffs of Dover to ask me what I—returning with no bones broken, so to speak—had done with my very young brother . . . (xxi.)

At this stage (Chapter v) when it is introduced, the phrase 'one of us' contains the possibilities of interpretation in limited ways—one of us seamen, one of us Englishmen, one of us gentlemen—at least, it has the notion of a restricted class. The second mention widens the reference a little, because it no longer applies to the 'us' who are assembled at Charley's, but to those we like to feel marching to left and right of us.

As they sit down to dinner at the Malabar Hotel, Marlow speaks of Jim's appearance:

> . . . all the time I had before me these blue, boyish eyes looking straight into mine, this young face, these capable shoulders, the open bronzed forehead with a

white line under the roots of the clustering fair hair, this
appearance appealing at sight to all my sympathies: this
frank aspect, the artless smile, the youthful seriousness.
He was of the right sort; he was one of us.            (vii.)

Now this appearance is to be measured by Marlow against
the reality and rejected; Jim is not to be trusted with 'a
deck'. But the 'right sort' acknowledges, as do Marlow
and Conrad both to the last, the bond. Here perhaps Jim
is being contrasted with the tourists from the outward-
bound mail-boat who are also eating at the Malabar; these
gross and unimpressible beings upon whom the Eastern
life has no more influence than have the baggage-labels
upon their trunks. Jim is not to be compared with them—
he at least knows what the influence of life, especially in
the heightened atmosphere of the Eastern seas, may be; he
has seen and experienced the decay of the 'lounger
through existence' as too the fear of the emergency which
paralyses.

The next mention of the phrase places it firmly in a
wider human context. Jim comes to stand for mankind:
his attitude towards the situation in the *Patna* for the
sides of human nature which face truth and falsehood;
only, in Jim's case the two are confounded. In a way which
Marlow does not understand, appearance and reality,
truth and falsehood are confounded and made to appear as
one. This shakes Marlow, and forces him to question his
own beliefs and attitudes. Jim, in his efforts towards self-
justification, rationalization, reconciliation of the shame of
the act with the height of his ideals, asks several times what
Marlow—or any other man—would have felt or done; or
else assumes that they would have done the same. The
most striking occurrence of this is when he asks Marlow:

'You don't think yourself a—a—cur?'
And with this—upon my honour!—he looked up at
me inquisitively. It was a question, it appears—a bona
fide question!                                          (vii.)

Marlow finds himself in danger of being 'circumvented,
bullied, perhaps, into taking a definite part in a dispute
impossible of decision if one had to be fair to all the
phantoms in possession—to the respectable that had its
claims and to the disreputable that had its exigencies'. (iii.)
In this world where the inconceivable is made comprehensible, Marlow's faith in the simple answer is shaken.
Now, this attempt on the part of Jim to involve Marlow
in his own failure is a neat turning of the tables in the
matter of this 'one of us'. What Jim is in effect doing is to
say that not only does he belong to the world of Marlow,
Charley and the others, with its standards and its successes,
but also they partake in his world, his shadowy existence
of denials of standards and of failures.

Marlow is swayed; swayed into seeing the mystery of
Jim's crime as an expression of universal fallibility.

The occasion was obscure, insignificant—what you
will: a lost youngster, one in a million—but then he
was one of us; an incident as completely devoid of
importance as the flooding of an ant-heap, and yet the
mystery of his attitude got hold of one as though he
had been an individual in the forefront of his kind, as if
the obscure truth involved were momentous enough to
affect mankind's conception of itself.          (vii.)

Here the concept of what is 'important', 'significant', is
called in question. As the eminently sensible world sees it,
can a truth so obscure have so large an effect? Is this view

of Marlow's valid? We should not, I think, rush to consider that because it posits a cosmic symbol this must be the truth of the matter. Conrad through Marlow in *Heart of Darkness* says that

> ... the meaning of an episode was not inside, like a kernel, but outside, enveloping the table which brought it out only as a glow brings out a haze, in the likeness of one of these misty haloes that sometimes are made visible by the spectral illumination of moonshine.

Moonshine, indeed! the scrupulously exact mediaeval allegorists might have muttered, seeing their favourite term for the hidden meaning (*nucleus*) thus swept aside. Indeed, this does not seem to offer much possibility of discovering meanings which can be stated adequately— compare also Jim's (and Marlow's) attitude to the Court's questions: 'so much to the point and so useless'. Are these attitudes to be accepted by us? Are we too meant to be swayed? I think not. There is throughout *Lord Jim* the sense of a double standard which plagues our judgement on Jim. There is the standard which is set up and expressed by such ideas as 'the craft'—and there is the standard which Jim, and occasionally Marlow too, acknowledges, namely this mystical meaning towards which Marlow is always striving. This latter standard, however, together with the world of conceptions which engender it, is seen to be insubstantial, the phantasmal product of the imaginative, the romantic mind which in the end ruins the man who abandons himself to it. Marlow's acknowledgement of its presence within man, and his elevation of it in this passage to the status of a constituent part of man, a cosmic principle, as it were, does not imply support of it. Conrad is in this sense no Romantic. Recognition he

certainly accords it, indeed presents it as a vital principle
in Jim; but he recognizes it only to warn against it. If Jim
be an 'individual in the forefront of his kind' it is as an
expression of that element in man which must be sup-
pressed, which must not be allowed to gain the upper
hand. This is explicitly brought out in the last mention of
the phrase 'one of us'—at the end of the book:

> He goes away from a living woman to celebrate his
> pitiless wedding with a shadowy ideal of conduct. Is he
> satisfied—quite, now, I wonder? We ought to know.
> He is one of us—and have I not stood up once, like an
> evoked ghost, to answer for his eternal constancy? Was
> I so very wrong after all? Now he is no more, there are
> days when the reality of his existence comes to me with
> an immense, with an overwhelming force; and yet upon
> my honour there are moments, too, when he passes
> from my eyes like a disembodied spirit astray among
> the passions of the earth, ready to surrender himself
> faithfully to his own world of shades.             (xlv.)

Here the two worlds are brought together, and the world
of Jim, 'the mist in which he moved and had his being'
(xi.) is shown as insubstantial and unreal; also as humanly
undesirable. If it was the 'exquisite sensibilities' of Jim
that caused Schomberg the inconvenience of sending to
Europe for a new billiard cue, it is here the 'shadowy ideal
of conduct' which causes the living woman, Jewel, to
enter into that 'soundless, inert life' which is a kind of
death of the spirit. Marlow says that it is the cause of the
call of his exalted egoism that tore him from Jewel's
jealous love. In this Jim represents that divisive spirit in
man that is to be shunned and guarded against. The 'place
of decay' is perhaps the place where a man seeks only his

G

own—whether it be his own comfort, in the comfortable deck-chairs and the distinction of being white—or his self-esteem, in getting shot for a shadowy ideal of personal heroism. The fierce glance to left and right appears as Jim's final vindication of himself to himself—for to the rest, to those who weigh his works and their effects, is he at all vindicated? The comparison with the Bob Stanton episode seems to suggest not—for Bob went down in an effort to save a lady's maid: but Jim's death was, like his jump, an effort to save himself.

By the time we come to this last use of the phrase within the novel, then, its import has broadened out into something like a statement of a human principle which is foreshadowed in the figure of Jim. The question remains as to whether we see him as an heroic figure, like the Wanderer of the Old English poem, Wolfram's Parzifal or Bunyan's Christian; or as an inflated and comic figure, like Cervantes' Don Quixote, or Melmoth the Wanderer, or Thurber's Walter Mitty. His kinship with us is stressed in his frailties, his dreams, his endeavours and his failures; in his attempts at self-justification we hear the voice of the indecisive man everywhere. In this, in the qualities of the human condition which he displays, if not in any overt and literal community, he is 'one of us'.

## Questions and Projects

1. *Lord Jim* may be said to belong to the literature of Quest: what would you say it is that Jim is seeking and do you think he found it?

2. In what ways can the Patusan close of the novel be said to be aesthetically right but morally ambiguous?

3. 'Jim is the victim not of moral weakness but of

imagination.' Develop fully your interpretation of this comment and say how far you agree with it.

4. Trace the use of the phrase 'one of us' through the novel and show how its significance changes by the close of the story.

5. Find out what authors are often said to have, like Conrad, 'a code' (e.g. Hemingway) and indicate how far their 'code' may be said to be akin to that of Conrad.

6. Prepare material to show how you would discuss the statements: (a) '*Lord Jim* is a masterpiece—but imperfect.' (b) 'Only those who recognize their own human imperfection can appreciate *Lord Jim*.' (c) '*Lord Jim* achieves the perfect balance of romance and realism.'

## 6. *LORD JIM* AND THE CRITICS

Criticism of Conrad and of his works is a sizeable industry, and a selection of some of the more important of the critical works for the study of *Lord Jim* will be found in the Bibliography. In addition to this, however, it is perhaps instructive to notice what earlier critics said about the novel on its first appearance. In his earlier years Conrad had on the whole an unfavourable press. *Lord Jim* was, however, received with more enthusiasm than its immediate predecessor, *The Nigger of the 'Narcissus'*, which many had found 'dull'. The novel was praised by the critics of the *Academy*, the *Speaker*, and the *Spectator*. The reviewers stressed the significance of local colour in Conrad's writing, and of the air of the exotic: the *Academy*, for example, said that Jim was 'one of those men who are engaged in relating the East to the West; those strange links with the two civilizations; voluntary exiles from this country, denationalising themselves that the British flag shall find trade wherever it penetrates'. Plainly the reviewer had failed to grasp the point of the novel, although the 'relating of the East to the West' was a lucky hit, though not in the sense in which the critic meant it. With more acumen, the *Outlook* said that *Lord Jim* combined the appeal for the reader of *Almayer's Folly* and *The Nigger of the 'Narcissus'*, and spoke of 'a wonderfully fascinating air of romance of the sea and of the mystery of the Orient'.

Nevertheless, what we should probably regard as the more literary aspects of the novel aroused dispute. The characterization was one of the points for which some critics took Conrad to task. The *Academy* was favourable to most of the characters, and their presentation, but could not accept Brierly's suicide. This is, perhaps, an interesting critical point from an otherwise mainly unilluminating article. It is plain that the suicide of Brierly is contrived by Conrad for the sake of the comparison which it enables him to make with the case of Jim, and to suggest that the distinction between success and failure as the world sees it may not be all that great when seen from the human and moral standpoint; but it may, indeed, be argued that as an incident in the novel it is somewhat strained in point of verisimilitude. As a coincidence, it may strike us as too neat. The *Academy* also found that the novel was 'a searching study—prosecuted with patience and understanding—of the cowardice of a man who was not a coward'. This may perhaps be brought to bear on the question which we were discussing earlier of the adequacy of terms. The *Bookman*, however, was confident that Jim was a coward; and also produced the curious remark: 'Is it well for us to be reminded that such persons may be as infinitely complicated, as civilisedly degenerate as any dweller in refined and sophisticated circles? We do not know. Mr Conrad may have written an unwise . . . book.' The *Bookman*'s reviewer attacked Conrad for being 'wrongly devoted to analysing the soul' in Jim. Now this kind of remark takes us outside the immediate context of criticism of the novel before us, and takes us into the more exalted realms of aesthetics and morality. Nevertheless, it is interesting as a contemporary reaction of disturbance at the reading of the novel, and shows that the significance of the novel in terms of the portrayal of man therein did not go unnoticed.

The narrative method aroused opposition, although most critics attacked it not on the grounds of its tortuosity so much as in terms of verisimilitude. The *Academy* considered that Conrad had made a mistake in turning the story over to Marlow to be told as an after-dinner story because such a long after-dinner conversation was 'an unacceptable convention' and Marlow's monologue was obviously written and not spoken. The critic Hugh Clifford, writing in the *North American Review*, felt also that the monologue was 'an illusion which it is impossible to sustain'. The *Athenaeum* found that the illusion was more successful in the serial form in which *Lord Jim* had originally appeared. The *Bookman* thought that the story was 'much too long' and that 'half of it should have been mercilessly sacrificed'. *The Speaker* however, defended Marlow's conversational monologue with some penetration: 'Marlow and the apparent artlessness of the narrative prevent the reader's becoming so absorbed in the action that he fails to perceive the meaning of the tale'. The *Critic* went into the structure in most detail, with a fascinating image:

> Imagine a fat, furry spider with green head and shining points for eyes, busily at work . . . on a marvellous web, and you have the plot of *Lord Jim*. It spins itself away, out of nothing, with side tracks leading, apparently, nowhere, and cross tracks that start back and begin anew and end once more—sometimes on the verge of nowhere, and sometimes in the centre of the plot itself . . .
>
> The completed web is a marvel of workmanship.

Conrad, of course, defends himself in the *Author's Note* to the 1917 edition against the charge of lack of verisimilitude, saying, '. . . all that part of the book which is Marlow's narrative can be read through aloud, I should say, in less than three hours'. But, as his subsequent remarks show, he plainly thought this criticism to be trivial. Indeed, few of the early remarks of the critics on the narrative technique are particularly penetrating. The *New York Tribune* defended the cohesion of the complete work, although it commented on the fact the original plan was for a short story, saying that 'the unpremeditated expansion to the form of a full-fledged novel has done nothing to spoil the simplicity and balance of the design'. Exactly what is meant here by 'unpremeditated' is not certain; it seems that Conrad's own words that 'a notion got about that I had been bolted away with' are regrettably true. Few seem to have seen the necessary connection of the parts of the novel; and the criticism of F. R. Leavis, which we shall note presently, has done much to fix this notion.

Although many critics perceived the excellence of the novel, few thought that it would prove popular. The *Spectator* said that *Lord Jim* was 'at once superlatively artistic in treatment and entirely original in its subject'. The *Academy* praised its 'poetical, romantic, half-wistful air . . . its application to life, to all of us' (which 'air' the *Speaker* characterized as 'the tricks of those who try to express more than they mean'.) Nevertheless, even the enthusiastic *Spectator* thought that it would hardly be popular:

Mr. Conrad's matter is too much detached from 'actuality' to please the great and influential section of readers who like their fiction to be spiced with topical allusions, political personalities, or the mondanities of

> Mayfair . . . Mr. Conrad, in a word, takes no heed of
> the vagaries of fashion of pseudo-culture . . .

The *Outlook* (like Marlow's host, Charley) thought that the
narrator was too subtle: 'the novel's qualities are of a
particularly refined and half-elusive kind which may well
prove unattractive to the multitude'. The *Critic* came up
with the not entirely obtuse prediction: 'If he keeps on
writing the same sort, he may arrive at the unique
distinction of having few readers in his own generation,
and a fair chance of several in the next'. But the *Bookman*
took a more gloomy view, on which we will conclude our
brief survey of the early critics:

> The novel is more than usually serious, more than
> usually depressing, and to such as are not psychological
> students . . . very tedious.

F. R. Leavis is a critic whose writings, in contrast to
those which we have just been considering, are generally
available, and indeed his writing on Conrad in his provo-
cative book *The Great Tradition* should be studied with
attention. He damns *Lord Jim*, and his pronouncement has
done much to mould the climate of critical opinion on the
work until recent years. He says that it 'doesn't deserve
the position of pre-eminence among Conrad's works often
assigned it'. He views the novel as inconsequential, as
broken-backed:

> The presentment of Lord Jim in the first part of the
> book, the account of the inquiry and of the desertion of
> the *Patna*, the talk with the French lieutenant—these
> are good Conrad. But the romance that follows, though
> plausibly offered as a continued exhibition of Jim's case,
> has no inevitability as that; nor does it develop or

enrich the central interest, which consequently, eked out to provide the substance of a novel, comes to seem decidedly thin.

Whether we agree with this finding or not depends on our view of the nature of the novel. Considered as narrative, as a 'yarn' Leavis's remarks are perhaps just acceptable, in much the same way as the criticism of Brierly's suicide as improbable is acceptable; but if we consider the novel to be more than that, to have the function of presenting, not so much an action or even a character but a moral meaning and a wider significance than that of the merely personal—if we think that Conrad is trying to say something rather about the human condition than about Augustine Podmore Williams, then I think we must see that Conrad has used all the devices of prose writing to convey this significance. Inevitability is here not narrative, but essentially moral.

## *Questions and Projects*:

1. It has been said that a novel is life looked at through a temperament. Accepting this as a basis develop an essay to show your sense of the temperament and attitude to life of Conrad as revealed in *Lord Jim*.

2. 'It is not action, but the springs of action in which Conrad is primarily interested.' Illustrate and discuss this comment with reference to either Jim or Brierly.

3. For what reasons do you think *Lord Jim* is, or is not, likely to be accepted as part of the literature of the novel?

4. Select a novel by a writer other than Conrad and make a collection of quotations about it from contemporary critical reviews.

5. Choose what seems to you a sound or illuminating

comment from those quoted in Ch. vi, illustrate and discuss it.

6. Collect evidence both to support and to oppose the general verdict passed by F. R. Leavis (as cited in Ch. vi) on *Lord Jim*.

# BIBLIOGRAPHY: SUGGESTIONS FOR
# FURTHER READING

I. WORKS OF CONRAD:

*Almayer's Folly*: A Story of an Eastern River.

*The Nigger of the 'Narcissus'*.

*Typhoon and other stories* (contains *Typhoon* and *Heart of Darkness*).

*Nostromo*.

These are all available in the collected edition of the *Complete Works of Joseph Conrad* published by Double-day, Doran & Co., 26 vols. (New York 1938).

II. CONRAD'S LIFE AND BACKGROUND STUDIES:

Allen, J. *The Sea Years of Joseph Conrad* (Methuen, London 1967).

Baines, J. *Joseph Conrad: A Critical Biography* (McGraw-Hill Book Co., New York 1960).

Ford, F. M. *Joseph Conrad: A Personal Remembrance* (Little, Brown & Co., Boston 1925).

Jean-Aubry, G. *Joseph Conrad: Life and Letters* (2 vols.) (Doubleday, Page & Co., New York 1927).

Sherry, N. *Conrad's Eastern World* (Cambridge University Press 1966).

III. SELECTED CRITICISM:

Guerard, A. J. *Conrad the Novelist* (Harvard University Press, Cambridge, Massachusetts 1958).

Hewitt, D. *Lord Jim: Conrad and the 'Few Simple Notions'* (in *Conrad: A Collection of Critical Essays*, ed. Mudrick). (Prentice-Hall, Inc., New Jersey 1966).

Leavis, F. *The Great Tradition*. (Chatto & Windus, London 1948; Peregrine Books 1967).

# NOTES ON ENGLISH LITERATURE

Chief Adviser: JOHN D. JUMP, *Professor of English Literature in the University of Manchester*

General Editor: W. H. MASON, *Sometime Senior English Master, The Manchester Grammar School*

1 Shakespeare **Macbeth**
JOHN HARVEY

2 Chaucer **The Prologue**
R. W. V. ELLIOTT, *Professor of English, Flinders University, South Australia*

3 T. S. Eliot **Murder in the Cathedral**
W. H. MASON

4 Austen **Pride and Prejudice**
J. DALGLISH, *Sometime Senior English Master, Tiffin School*

5 Shakespeare **Twelfth Night**
BARBARA HARDY, *Professor of English, Royal Holloway College*

7 Emily Brontë **Wuthering Heights**
BARBARA HARDY

8 Hardy **The Mayor of Casterbridge**
G. G. URWIN, *Senior English Master, Sale Grammar School for Boys*

9 Charlotte Brontë **Jane Eyre**
BARBARA HARDY

10 Shaw **St. Joan**
W. H. MASON

11 Conrad **Nostromo**
C. B. COX, *Professor of English Literature, University of Manchester*

12 Dryden **Absalom and Achitophel**
W. GRAHAM, *Sometime Senior English Master, Dame Allan's Boys' School, Newcastle-upon-Tyne*

13 Sheridan **The Rivals, The School for Scandal, The Critic**
B. A. PHYTHIAN, *Senior English Master, The Manchester Grammar School*

14 Shakespeare **King Lear**
HELEN MORRIS, *Principal Lecturer in English, Homerton College, Cambridge*

15 Forster **A Passage to India**
W. H. MASON

16 Chaucer · · · · **The Nun's Priest's Tale and the Pardoner's Tale**
R. W. V. ELLIOTT

17 Milton · · · · · · **Paradise Lost, Books IV and IX**
W. GRAHAM

18 Shakespeare · · **King Richard II**
HELEN MORRIS

19 Browning · · · · **Men and Women**
MARK ROBERTS, *Professor of English Literature, University of Belfast*

20 Webster · · · · · **The White Devil, The Duchess of Malfi**
JOHN D. JUMP, *Professor of English Literature, University of Manchester*

21 George Eliot · · · **Middlemarch**
A. O. COCKSHUT, *Fellow of Hertford College, Oxford*

22 Shakespeare · · **The Winter's Tale**
G. P. FOX, *Lecturer in English, Department of Education, University of Exeter*

23 Lawrence · · · · **Sons and Lovers**
CHRISTOPHER HANSON, *Lecturer in English Literature, University of Manchester*

24 Mrs. Gaskell · · **Sylvia's Lovers**
GRAHAM HANDLEY, *Senior Lecturer in English, All Saints' College, Tottenham*

25 Shakespeare · · **Antony & Cleopatra**
HELEN MORRIS

26 Wordsworth · · **The Prelude I & II**
W. GRAHAM

27 Forster · · · · · **Howards End**
G. P. WAKEFIELD, *Senior English Master, King George V School, Southport*

28 Austen · · · · · **Persuasion**
J. R. COATES, *Senior English Master, Hymer's College, Kingston-upon-Hull*

29 Woolf · · · · · · **To the Lighthouse**
W. A. DAVENPORT, *Lecturer in English, Royal Holloway College*

30 Shaw · · · · · · **Man and Superman**
A. W. ENGLAND, *Senior Lecturer in English, Eaton Hall College of Education, Retford, Notts.*

31 Synge · · · · · · **Riders to the Sea, Playboy of the Western World**
A. PRICE, *Senior Lecturer in Education, Queen's University, Belfast*

32 Byron · · · · · · **Childe Harold III and IV, Vision of Judgement**
PATRICIA BALL, *Lecturer in English, Royal Holloway College*

33 Shakespeare · · **Othello**
G. P. WAKEFIELD

34 Dickens · · · · · **Bleak House**
P. DANIEL, *Assistant Master, Ratcliffe College, Leicester*